To Drink of His Love

To Drink of His Love

MARY F. WUESTEFELD

REVIEW AND HERALD PUBLISHING ASSOCIATION
Washington, DC 20039-0555
Hagerstown, MD 21740

This book was
Edited by Gerald Wheeler
Designed by Richard Steadham
Type set: 11/12 Zapf

PRINTED IN U.S.A.

Library of Congress Cataloging in Publication Data

Wuestefeld, Mary F., 1954-
To drink of his love.

1. Wuestefeld, Mary F., 1954- . 2. Converts, Seventh-day Adventist—United States—Biography. I. Title.
BX6193.W84A34 1986 248.2'46'0924 [B] 85-19440
ISBN 0-8280-0312-2

CONTENTS

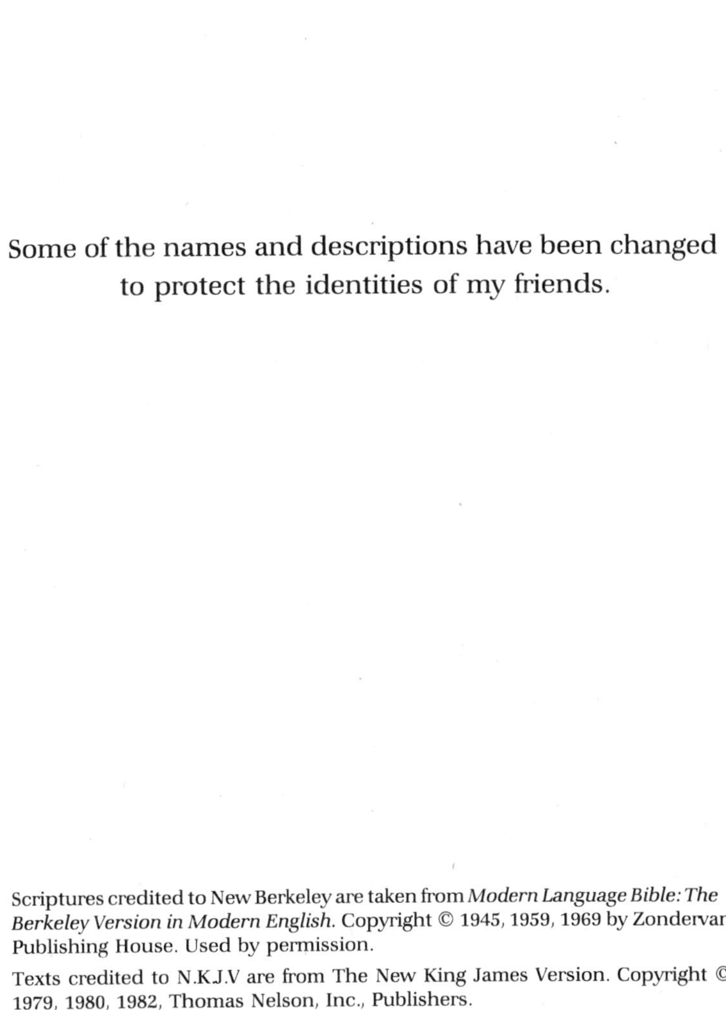

Some of the names and descriptions have been changed to protect the identities of my friends.

"He who seeks to quench his thirst at the fountains of this world will drink only to thirst again. Everywhere men are unsatisfied. They long for something to supply the need of the soul. Only One can meet that want. The need of the world, 'The Desire of all nations,' is Christ. The divine grace which He alone can impart is as living water, purifying, refreshing, and invigorating the soul."

—*Ellen G. White*

1

DREAMING

"It shall come to pass, that before they call, I will answer" (Isaiah 65:24).

Morning classes over, I lay drowsily on my bed thinking about my life, my future. I knew I was searching for something. All my life I had been seeking something more, and now, in my sophomore year at college, the yearning in my heart was intensifying. As I pondered my existence I drifted off into a short catnap.

Suddenly I found myself on a beautiful shoreline walking along a white sandy beach and wading in water bluer than any I'd ever seen before. I sensed some awesome power in the midst of the land and marveled at the heavenly surroundings.

While strolling along the beach, I beheld a dazzling sight. Not far from me a sparkling golden vase covered with jewels of the most brilliant hues shimmered in the sun. Never had I seen such a beautiful object. As I walked toward the vase and began to reach for it, a voice—not an audible one, but a voice touching my innermost being—began to speak.

"In this vase you will find one golden drop of pure love. It is your task to spread this love to all you meet."

"One drop of love!" I exclaimed to myself. How could I spread just one drop of love around to everybody in such a vast world?

Days, weeks, and years passed by in my dream as I struggled to find some way of sharing that one pure drop of love. But every method I tried failed. Then, in my despair, that strong, gentle voice spoke to my heart once again.

"The secret, my child, is to drink the drop yourself. Then you will succeed."

In awe and wonder I pondered this remarkable advice. Then my dream faded and I awoke once again in the drab little room of the century-old two-story house where I resided.

2

A PAINFUL ENDING

*"In the hearts of all mankind, of whatever race or station in life, there are inexpressible longings for something they do not now possess."**

My parents and I chatted cheerfully over salads in a local restaurant near the University of California campus where I still attended school. A year and a half had now passed since my dream about the drop of love. My need to discover a deeper meaning in life, along with difficult circumstances at school, had brought me to a crisis point—but neither I nor my parents knew what dramatic changes would soon take place.

Spending a day with my parents always helped me to feel more optimistic. My job as editor in chief of our university newspaper was not going as well as I had hoped, and I sensed that a few key staff members were plotting some kind of power play. Because of my intense devotion to the newspaper, my grades had plummeted, and academic probation seemed imminent. Despite all this, my parents encouraged me, and near the end of our meal my father scribbled something on his coffee-stained napkin. As he handed it to me I read, "It is always darkest just before the dawn." "The mills of the gods grind slowly but exceedingly fine." "Whom the gods will destroy they first make mad with power."

As I contemplated the familiar quotations I wondered if the light really was about to break forth for me. Could the personality problems I was facing at the newspaper be smoothed out soon? Could I find a solution for my ailing grades? Even more important, could the deep inner emptiness I had been experiencing for so long ever be filled? This question had now become paramount, and the problems I faced at school seemed small in comparison. I hungered for some solutions to the unspoken questions in my life concerning my existence and my future.

My parents and I parted shortly after witnessing a magnificent rainbow arching across the northern California sky. I felt a strange premonition that I was on the verge of something awesome, but I had no idea that it would be the last time I would see my mother and father for almost fourteen months.

Things didn't get much better. The power struggle between my staff and I became more intense, my academic situation continued downward, and the emptiness within only grew deeper.

One evening, as I was covering an important political campaign for our county, one of the candidates accused me of unfair campaign coverage. It seemed absurd to me because, to tell the truth, I could not have cared less which one of the candidates got elected. Politics was not one of my major interests, although I feigned concern for my job's sake.

That same evening my city news editor started criticizing my editorial writing. He was a mature, married man about ten years my senior and, although I didn't know it then, interested in my job. After convincing me that I should go home and get some sleep, he took over for the rest of the night.

As I walked into my lonely little apartment, frustration welled up inside me. I had counted so much on this job to fill the void in my heart, thinking that perhaps the prestige of the editorship and the journalistic clout that accompanied it would bring satisfaction. Instead, I was being accused and criticized and any so-called friends I had might as well have been enemies. In fact, my "best friend" wasn't even speaking to me because she disagreed with some of my policies at the newspaper.

Throwing myself down on the bed, I tried to cry, but the tears wouldn't come. I felt only a dry ache deep within me. Again, I began pondering my existence and wondering what I was accomplishing with my life. Especially I questioned whether or not there was anything or anyone who could truly fill my hungry soul and make the agony in my heart go away.

As I lay on my bed, suddenly an idea began to surface—an idea that at first seemed impossible but soon gripped me and brought hope back to my troubled mind. Why not leave this life behind and begin a journey to seek something better? I thought to myself. It would mean abandoning my job, my education, and my family, but as I contemplated the possibility, my heart donned wings. If there were something more to life, then I had to find it. I could no longer go on living a purposeless existence, nor could I continue piling experiences onto the surface of my life without discovering that which made them truly meaningful.

That evening I made my decision. I would follow my dream about the golden drop of love.

I cannot fully explain why a feeling of emptiness had been so prominent in my life. Some perceptive individual once proposed that "Within the heart of every person is a God-shaped vacuum that only He can fill."

From my earliest memories I was aware of something greater than myself in the universe, and as I grew older, a yearning to discover what or who that was continued to dominate me, becoming more pressing as I entered my teenage years. I came from a loving home but not a religious one, so I never seriously explored religion, although my thoughts did often turn to the possibility of

God.

At 5 years of age I can recall my father reading poems by my bedside. During such times I felt aware of a special power beyond us, but my childish thoughts could only experience the sensation, not begin to understand it.

When I was 9 my family took a vacation to Yellowstone National Park. While exploring the woods near our cabin, I felt the awesomeness of something greater than me. In response to it I wrote: "Through the woods I walk and wander/ Through the woods I pause and ponder/ Through the woods I walk so far/ Until I see the sun afar." Little did I know how appropriately those simple words described my future.

At 12 I pondered my existence in another poem: "Who are we?/ Are we clouds floating/ On the idea of life?/ Is this world a dream, a wish/ From someone else?/ Are we a flame/ flickering in the darkness/ Waiting for a distant wind/ to blow us out?"

And then at 16 I lamented my ever-deepening feeling that I had not yet found the answer to my longing:

"I am bound to society, stapled to the life of someone else's world. Traditions of yesterday hold me down as I struggle to gasp just one breath of my life. I take hold of my life, but society pries it away from me, leaving me torn between two lives, theirs and mine, fading into one another, indistinguishable as two . . . I want to break through! I want to gather all of me and burst through to my world! But I feel protected here, and I cannot find the courage. Oh, God! Give me the courage. I can't go on living the two lives, being ground to a nothing between the hideous walls, going nowhere in an endless hallway, wanting desperately to open a door and discover me inside. Give me the strength to hurl myself away from the clutches of them into the world of my reality filling the cavity in my soul."

I share these memories simply to illustrate that my

longing for something more in life did not merely arise out of a set of bad circumstances, but had long been a part of me. My decision to leave school and begin my quest, although activated by my difficult situation, did not result from the problems I was facing. Instead, it grew out of an ever-deepening need to fill that "cavity" within.

The decision was easy, but the pain of saying Goodbye to my college life was not so easy to take. Fortunately, I quickly and smoothly made the necessary arrangements for my departure. Incredibly, I sublet my apartment the very first afternoon I advertised it. Hurriedly I sold enough possessions to secure a one-way plane ticket to the Midwest after my brother, who was attending medical school in Michigan, offered to let me stay with him for a short while. I announced my resignation at the newspaper and withdrew from school without any complications. It seemed as though an unseen power cleared all obstacles. Even so, I could not avoid the pain of saying Goodbye to my family and to the job that had taken so much energy and determination to attain.

The most difficult aspect of my decision to leave school was thinking about the distress I would cause my parents when they found out. They had been so proud of my position as editor. Though I had decided not to tell them until my arrival in Michigan, they found out anyway, and the evening before I left we had a painful conversation by phone.

I also felt torn up over leaving the university newspaper that had virtually been my life for more than two years. When I announced my resignation and found out that most of my staff really had been behind me (only two or three key people were involved in the power struggle), I hesitated for a few uncertain moments, wondering if I were making a mistake. I reminded myself, however, that even if I could solve the problems at the newspaper, my feelings of emptiness would still remain, though they might be glossed over for a little while longer.

Another difficulty I faced was the sense of uncertainty concerning where I was headed. I knew I was going to Michigan to visit my brother indefinitely, but how would I cope with a totally new environment? Where would I live and how would I support myself? Still, the strength of conviction that I should begin this journey carried me through my most insecure moments.

Within two weeks I boarded a 727 jetliner, bound for Ann Arbor, Michigan, where I would begin my new life and my search for what I labeled "love." As the plane soared above the little college town and headed eastward, I felt a great sense of relief and expectation. "Help me, God, whoever or whatever You are, to find this love, this meaning to my life that I've been seeking so long" was my silent prayer.

3

MY LONELIEST CHRISTMAS

"He brought me up also out of an horrible pit, out of the miry clay" (Psalm 40:2).

Shortly after my arrival in Ann Arbor I located an apartment and found a minimum-wage job in an ice-cream parlor. My brother and I didn't see each other much, for he was busy as a medical student. Besides, we had an agreement that I should be on my own during this period of my life except for emergencies. (And, bless his heart, he did faithfully come through on my behalf in many times of emotional and financial need.)

The first friend I found after arriving in Michigan turned out to be a gay alcoholic who shared my lot of scooping out endless varieties of ice cream eight hours a day. After work, Milo and I frequented the bars together and drank ourselves into oblivion. I really didn't care about his sexual persuasion or alcoholism; he was someone I could talk to, and I desperately needed human companionship.

Milo was interested in the occult, and through him I found out about the Abra Cadabra House. Here I had my fortune told in the hopes of finding clues to my search, but I only got vague generalities about "light" and "darkness" on my path. Sometimes Milo and I conducted seances in which he would summon "Lucifer." Fortunately, Lucifer never showed up. It wasn't until months later that I found out who Lucifer was according to the Bible.

My friend and I began drinking together more and more. Since neither of us had anywhere to go for

Christmas, we made plans to spend the holiday together with our favorite "maddog" wine—an especially potent drink.

On Christmas Eve I decided to tour Main Street to catch a glimpse of Ann Arbor's Christmas decorations. I thought that perhaps this would cheer me up and give me a sense of the Christmas "spirit" I so longed for. As a youngster I had always gleefully anticipated the coming of Christmas, and now I sought to recapture a bit of the feeling.

Even the ornaments and tinsel displayed in the store windows didn't give me a lift, however, and once again I pondered the meaning and purpose of life. Wasn't Christmas supposed to be the season of love? Where was all of it? I noticed a woman sounding rushed and irritable to a store clerk. "So much for the Christmas spirit," I said to myself; then I wandered home to spend my first Christmas Eve alone.

Christmas morning Milo arrived bright and early, and we broke open the "maddog" right away. We celebrated the holiday by discussing the hypocrisy of it all as we downed our favorite drink. Milo and I were quite adept at tearing things down, but we never seemed to come up with anything constructive. Instead we simply kept each other company in the "pit."

At some point during the morning my parents called to wish me Merry Christmas. I don't know how much wine I had put away by that time, but I think I managed to have a normal conversation and sound cheerful. It was good to hear their friendly voices and to know that someone really cared for me. Our conversation was the only bright spot in my Christmas that year. The rest of the day is merely a blur in my memory.

After Christmas I felt sad that I had not captured the spirit of the season. I feared that the "spirit of Christmas," or spirit of love that everyone talked about, was impossible for me to grasp. Always, like a bubble, it popped before I could catch it. By next Christmas season I hoped that something would be different and that this elusive spirit of love would be mine.

4

LOOKING FOR LOVE

"The heart yearns for human love, but this love is not strong enough, or pure enough, or precious enough, to supply the place of the love of Jesus." *

New Year's Eve found me in a restaurant with a new friend named Rob. He and I met a few days after Christmas while dancing at a disco. Typical of the way my heart usually worked, I thought I was madly in love already.

A weight lifter and health enthusiast, Rob didn't drink liquor, but bought me a few fancy concoctions while we dined. I felt so fortunate to have such a wonderful New Year's Eve companion, and my hope that maybe a good relationship with him was just beginning soared.

My new friend was an interesting yet somewhat mysterious person. (Later I discovered that he was a drug dealer.) He told me that he was searching too—although he wasn't sure for what. At one point he asked me rather hesitantly, "Have you ever wondered who God is?"

His question took me off guard. Yes, I had often wondered who God is, but at the moment I didn't really feel like discussing it. Frankly, I was more interested in Rob. "I think God is someone who looks down at earth and laughs at the big mess we've gotten ourselves into," I flippantly answered. Rob laughed slightly and inquired no more.

Later I bemoaned the fact that I had not pursued our conversation further. I really would like to have explored the subject of God with my friend, and I wondered why I had given such a shallow reply when he brought it up. Probably the mixed drinks had dulled my senses. As it turned out, I never got a chance to hear his opinion, for shortly after New Year's Eve he dropped me like a hot potato, crushing my hopes for our relationship.

Toward the end of January I lost my job at the ice-cream store for drinking on the premises after work. The store also fired Milo, and from then on we didn't see so much of each other. Rob's health habits had impressed me, and I gradually cut down on my drinking, so Milo and I didn't have as much in common anymore.

Fortunately I found a new job a few days later at a fancy restaurant down the street from the ice-cream parlor. Once again, I plummeted headfirst into infatuation, this time with one of the cooks.

Paul and I took a liking to each other right away. He was tall, blond, and very outgoing. We took long walks in the snow-covered arboretum while discussing the meaning of life and love. It wasn't long before he said that he loved me.

For a few weeks everything went well. The world about me seemed new, fresh, and alive, and I wondered if this was what I had come all the way from California to find.

And then it happened. Suddenly Paul went from hot to cold. After I arrived at his home one evening, he seemed strangely distant. Then, to my utter dismay, he said that he no longer loved me and that I wasn't for him, and he wanted me to leave immediately. (Later I discovered that Paul already had a serious girlfriend and that I was just a fling.) Outside a blizzard was blowing, and I owned no transportation. He didn't even offer to take me home. My heart fell to a new depth.

The pain I felt was overwhelming. It was as if all of the heartbreaks that I had ever experienced now came rushing into my memory full-force, extinguishing every bit of hope for a future love. Was my life just some cruel joke that held love out to me like a carrot on a stick and then snatched it away before I could get it? Was heartbreak destined to be the story of my existence?

My problems with romance had begun in about the tenth grade when I found my first serious boyfriend. Our relationship didn't last long, however, and I ended up dating a variety of people throughout my high school days. Heartbreak was almost always the result, either on my end or theirs, for I never seemed to click with the right one.

Then, during the summer before my freshman year in college, I fell seriously in love with Andrew. By the time fall rolled around we were engaged, and I was ecstatic. But because we were both too selfish to understand the real meaning of love, it wasn't long before our relationship began to deteriorate. Our constant bickering over differing views left little room for individuality and smothered the romantic feelings that had once flourished so abundantly. Still, our relationship hung on for several months. Argue as we did, we were too attached to each other to end our association.

It finally became apparent that we would never work out our differences, so my boyfriend made the final break just one year after proposing marriage. Because so many of my hopes and dreams had centered upon my fiancé, I felt as though the ending of the relationship had ripped out part of my heart.

The following two years brought a series of heartbreaks. One relationship after another failed, either because of my disinterest or theirs. (It wasn't until many years later that I fully understood why I had met with such difficulty in establishing good relationships with the opposite sex—the main reasons being my selfishness and insecurity.) Romance kept me in constant turmoil, and I never seemed to realize that by placing so many of my hopes in men I was bound to be hurt.

But after my rejection by Paul, I finally saw that the pathway of romantic love just wasn't reliable and certainly wasn't meeting my deepest heartfelt needs. I temporarily made a conscious decision to avoid falling in love, and to turn my eyes more seriously toward spiritual matters. It was finally becoming clear that I must seek a love more than human in order to satisfy my heart's deepest longings.

5

EARTHRIDERS

*"The warmth of true friendship . . . is a foretaste of the joys of heaven."**

Fortunately, after my friendship with Milo ended, a new friend came into my life. Mary, a downstairs neighbor of mine, was someone with whom I could share my innermost thoughts.

Her Catholic background and belief in the Bible didn't really bother me, although I felt beyond that sort of thing. She liked to philosophize about life as much as I, and we spent hours contemplating our existence. Mary's love for nature often brought us to the arboretum, and sometimes when we sat on the grassy slopes we would imagine ourselves riding swiftly through the universe on the sphere called earth. Thus, we called ourselves "earthriders."

The name "earthriders" meant more than just global travelers. It symbolized our common desire to understand what our journey on earth was all about. Mary often spoke about God, and sometimes even shared Scripture verses with me. Though I didn't believe in the Bible, I felt an incredible peace when she read from it, a reaction I marveled at.

One day she said something that really startled me. We were sitting in my apartment listening to one of my favorite record albums when a song with the following words came on: "Baby, I'm through/ running, it's true/ I'd be a fool/ to try and escape you/ No more retreat/ only a sweet surrender." After I expressed my delight in the sentimental lyrics, Mary looked at me seriously and said,

"Do you know what that song means to me? . . . Those words speak of my surrender to God."

Taken off guard by her comment, I felt strangely ill at ease. Always when listening to that particular song, I had envisioned a beautiful love affair in which some dashing young man fell madly in love with me. And here Mary was thinking about God! I tried to ignore her comment, but it lodged itself uncomfortably in my subconscious.

At times Mary's statement about "surrendering to God" came into my mind, and it positively scared me. In my limited understanding of God, I felt that to surrender to Him—whoever or whatever He was—meant to give up everything enjoyable in life. I had no idea what one might gain from a surrender except, perhaps, some sort of pious self-satisfaction in feeling "holy" enough to make that kind of sacrifice, or maybe, if one was lucky, some kind of incredible supernatural experience. Besides, surrendering to someone or something that I didn't know much about was downright frightening. Still, I couldn't get rid of a nagging feeling every time her words echoed in my mind.

One day Mary asked if I'd like to stop in at a little brick church near our apartments for a short time of prayer and meditation. This particular church was open twenty-four hours a day for anyone feeling a need. The atmosphere was so quiet and beautiful that I felt at peace as soon as I arrived.

At the front of the sanctuary, behind the podium, hung a portrait of Jesus. I gazed wonderingly into the artist's beautiful portrayal of His gentle face and transparent character, and felt myself strangely drawn toward Him. From that time on I made it a practice to stop in occasionally and lift my thoughts heavenward.

Several weeks into our friendship Mary gave me a small green pocketbook version of the New Testament. I didn't use it, but kept it on my dresser as a token of our friendship and common quest. Occasionally I wondered if the book did contain some clues to my search after all—why else would so many people refer to it as "God's Word"?

One evening as I sat fingering through the little Bible, I challenged God. Please, I prayed silently, tell me something about this Book, about Yourself, about my future. With that, I closed my eyes and let the pages fall open randomly. To my astonishment, as I opened my eyes, I saw this moving passage:

"Even though I speak in human and angelic language and have no love, I am as noisy brass or a clashing cymbal. And although I have the prophetic gift and see through every secret and through all that may be known, and have sufficient faith for the removal of mountains, but I have no love, I am nothing. And though I give all my belongings to feed the hungry and surrender my body to be burned, but I have no love, I am not in the least benefited.

"Love endures long and is kind; love is not jealous; love is not out for display; it is not conceited or unmannerly; it is neither self-seeking nor irritable, nor does it take account of a wrong that is suffered. . . . It bears everything in silence, has unquenchable faith, hopes under all circumstances, endures without limit.

"Love never fails. . . . Make love your great quest" (1 Corinthians 13:1-8, 14:1, New Berkeley).

As I read, I felt sure that the Bible had opened to this particular chapter by no mere coincidence. After all, wasn't genuine love just what I was looking for? Although I didn't read my Bible again for several weeks, I treasured the experience and pondered its significance.

My friendship with Mary flourished, even though we didn't see eye to eye on everything. Despite the peace I felt as she read scriptures to me, despite the drawing I felt as I gazed at the portrait of Jesus, and despite the impressive "love chapter" in the Bible, I still saw no point in becoming a Christian. I regarded these experiences only as clues to some other ultimate discovery beyond the realms of Christianity. My agnostic background yielded within me a strong aversion to allying myself with the Christian church, and I could not stomach the thought of becoming a "Jesus freak."

Fortunately, Mary didn't come on strong about her religious beliefs, but just interjected them politely every once in a while. We also spent a lot of time discussing people, poetry, and dreams. Our friendship was a great blessing to me, and the joy of communicating with a true friend fed my hungry soul. Relating to another human being on a spiritual level touched the vacuum inside, and yet I knew there was more, much more, for me to discover.

As I thought of the love and warmth that friendship brings, I felt that there must be a great Source somewhere containing an endless supply. I longed to discover it, for I knew all too well that human relationships end, and I hoped to discover something or someone totally reliable.

I began praying more—pouring my heart out to somebody, somewhere, who could understand my need. My greatest prayer was that God might reveal Himself to me and lead me into His truth and love. Little did I realize how faithfully and how patiently He was answering my heartfelt requests.

It wasn't long before Mary left for summer vacation, and my apartment lease ran out. My funds were running low, so all I could afford was a musty little room in a two-story house near the student section of town. My brother helped me with the rent deposit, and I moved my single battered suitcase into my new "home." Peanut-butter sandwiches and orange juice became my mainstay as I waited anxiously for another clue in my quest.

6

THE MAN THEY CALLED HOLY

"For false christs and false prophets will rise and show signs and wonders to deceive, if possible, even the elect" (Mark 13:22, N.K.J.V.).

In high school one of my favorite books was a famous work by Kahlil Gibran entitled *The Prophet*. The thoughts it expressed about love and life deeply touched me and helped to strengthen my desire to seek something more in the spiritual realm.

Now I decided to explore the Eastern religions. I bought books on the subject and began attending a meditation group started by an Indian Yogi named Muktananda. (Muktananda, proselytizing in the United States since 1974, has claimed at least twenty thousand devotees and has received visits from such prominent figures as former governor Jerry Brown, singer James Taylor, astronaut Edgar Mitchell, and singer Carly Simon.)[1]

Because the Eastern writings and meditation group so frequently mentioned the words *light* and *love,* I felt sure that I was on the verge of some answers for my life. It thrilled me when I heard that our spiritual leader, Muktananda, would be in New York for several weeks holding seminars and meditation gatherings, and I determined to meet this "holy" man.

According to some of Muktananda's followers, a person measures the quality of his spiritual life by the level he reaches while meditating. For instance, as a sign of initial progress, a devotee might see a white light before his eyes. Then, as he continues to grow, a "kriya" could come upon him. (A kriya is, supposedly, a shock of divine energy running down the spine that causes the meditator to shiver and shake and make strange noises.) A real sign of spiritual attainment occurs when the light changes to blue.

Having experienced neither the white light nor the kriya in the short time I had been meditating, I hoped that Muktananda might help me. I was told that simply through his touch one could experience a kriya, and a shock of divine energy sounded like just what I needed.

To my delight, I found a ride to New York with the brother of a young man who lived in my apartment house. David happened to attend the same meditation group as I, and offered to take me along to see the great "teacher."

Full of anticipation, we arrived at Muktananda's "ashram" (meditation house) on a warm July afternoon. Two thousand other seekers were milling around, and the air was charged with electricity. As a tour guide showed me the grounds he commented enthusiastically, "All of this has come through Baba's grace." (Baba is the Indian word for father and is also the endearing term used by Muktananda's followers.) He then went on to express how he felt spiritually married to Muktananda and completely satisfied in his love.

The tour guide was not the only one to profess total consecration to this man. During the course of my visit I saw men and women fall prostrate at his feet in humble adoration, and one new husband commented, "Before I married my wife, I married Muktananda."

Though I admired such devotion (and even longed for it toward Something or Somebody greater than myself), the more I observed Muktananda, the harder it became to envision him as the kind of man worthy of such veneration. According to Baba's followers, he had reached the highest spiritual level available to man—but some of his actions made me wonder.

During a wedding service in which he married several couples, a joke he told about an unfortunate individual who unveiled an ugly woman for a bride left me aghast. The anecdote seemed especially inappropriate for a "holy" man to share and certainly was not something that I would picture God saying at a wedding.

Then I heard he displayed irritability when things weren't done exactly to his liking. I couldn't imagine impatience in a man perfectly at one with the universe. Of course, his devotees explained his irritation as "righteous indignation."

When asked about his identity, Muktananda replied, "I am however you see me. If you see me as a saint, I am a saint. If you see me as a fool, I am a fool. If you see me as an ordinary man, I am an ordinary man."[2] This comment did not strike me as an enthusiastic profession of divinity. The more I learned of Muktananda, the less he fit my picture of God.

When Muktananda touched me with his peacock feather during the third day of my visit, I felt absolutely nothing. And a few hours later, as I sat amid hundreds of followers who were meditating, shivering, and occasionally screaming, I asked myself, "What am I doing here?" Disappointed that the trip had not furthered my spiritual quest, I left for Michigan that evening.

The following days, as I pondered Muktananda and his teachings, a few things especially bothered me. First of all, he charged what I thought were extravagant prices for "instant enlightenment" seminars in which he offered to transmit "shakti" (spiritual energy) in a matter of two short days. The fee was $100 and included only modest room and board. (I did not attend this particular seminar because of finances.) Anyone who would peddle instant spirituality made me suspicious.

Second, his philosophy always emphasized an inner delving rather than an outward seeking. "Meditate on yourself. Honor and worship your inner being. God dwells within you as you."[3] Meditating on myself hadn't gotten me anything but misery so far in my life, and I wanted Something or Someone outside of myself to show the way.

Another thing that made me leery was the fact that I saw few spiritual fruits, other than kriyas, among his followers. True, some of them experienced "flashing lights, visions, ethereal sounds,"[4] but what about such things as peace, joy, gentleness, and love? All his followers talked about love, but among his meditation group in Michigan I saw little of it actually displayed.

After the New York trip I found a book at the local ashram written by Muktananda. I hoped that by reading it I could gain some insights into his real person. But the more I read, the more I became certain that his group was not what I was asking for.

In one particular chapter, "Baba" described one of his secrets to a great spiritual life. He propounded that abstinence from sex (although his followers engaged in premarital sex with his consent) could tremendously enhance one's spiritual experience. He explained that as a man abstains from sexual intercourse, he stores spiritual energy within him.

This made no sense to me, for I couldn't believe that a person's spiritual life could hinge upon some sort of biological energy stored up as a result of refraining from sex. Instead, I had concluded that our spiritual lives are vitally bound up in our quest to know and become one with a God outside ourselves—a God of love. Besides, I believed that sex (as experienced within marriage) is a beautiful gift from God and does not detract from but rather enhances one's spirituality when enjoyed within the boundaries of God's principles.

The more I contemplated the books I had been exploring on Eastern religion and the more I thought about my experience with Muktananda, the more I realized that Eastern religion was not the answer to my great quest. Three main reasons became apparent to me.

The first, as I've mentioned already, is the emphasis on self-realization so prominent in Eastern thought. I couldn't believe that the answers I was searching for simply lay hidden within me waiting for some fantastic meditation experience to draw them out. If that was my only hope, then I felt there was no hope at all. No, I longed for Someone greater than I to teach me, to draw me close, to pour love into my thirsty heart.

Second, the teachings in Eastern religion may sound beautiful, but in reality they are abstract and hard to apply to one's practical life. The ethereal truths gave me a lift for a time as I meditated upon them, but left me with nothing to work with in the long run. I needed practical principles with which to enhance my everyday life, not just white lights and kriyas.

The third factor involved the absence of real heart transformation among Muktananda's followers and other Eastern devotees whom I observed. While professing spirituality, they often seemed no different than the average person when it came to courtesy, love, and peace of mind. I was seeking the kind of God, the kind of love, that could change my heart and life in a dynamic, invigorating way, making me altogether a new person.

Although I continued to visit the local ashram once in a while for a quiet time of meditation, my visits became more and more infrequent. Instead I began praying ever more intensely that the real God would soon reveal Himself.

7

FROM CURSING TO CHRIST

"It is God's design that [the] longing of the human heart should lead to the One who alone is able to satisfy it. The desire is of Him that it may lead to Him, the fullness and fulfillment of that desire. That fullness is found in Jesus Christ, the Son of the Eternal God."[1]

Near the end of my adventure with Eastern religion I noticed an interesting young man visiting a neighbor in my apartment house quite frequently. Mark sported a long, frizzy afro and a big smile—both of which caught my eye. From what I saw of him, he seemed like a gentle and mild-mannered person, and the few times I spoke with him he was courteous and kind. Needless to say, he impressed me.

One day I glanced out my window and, to my amazement, saw him pulling up in his little orange sports car piled high with suitcases, boxes, and a few pieces of furniture. After inquiring, I discovered that he was moving in with my next-door neighbor because his former roommate had skipped out on him and left him with an impossible rent payment. Secretly, I felt overjoyed at his arrival, for my intuition told me that Mark and I could become good friends.

It didn't take long for me to confirm my suspicion. The very first evening Mark moved in, we found ourselves conversing about our lives into the wee hours of the morning. By the time we retired to our respective rooms for the night, I knew I had discovered another friend, another seeker with whom to share my journey.

During the next few weeks we continued to converse about such topics as world events and supernatural experiences, and to express our common desire to turn from the ordinary and discover something deeper in life. Our friendship continued to grow and prosper—until one hot August evening when something happened that almost shattered it.

Coming home from work one afternoon, I noticed Mark sitting on the front porch intensely absorbed in some sort of book with a plain black cover. As I looked more closely I couldn't believe my eyes. He was studying the Bible.

This really surprised me. Mark hadn't mentioned the Bible or Christianity in our discussions, and because I still didn't have much regard for this particular piece of literature (even after my experience with Mary), I wondered what he found so intriguing inside those pages.

Plopping myself down on the porch, I began to question him about his choice of reading material. I don't remember exactly how it happened, but suddenly we found ourselves in the midst of a heated disagreement over the authenticity of the Bible.

"Don't you know that truth transcends the Bible?" I said vehemently. Mark remained calm, and expressed his new conviction that the Bible contained the ultimate truth for mankind. (Later I discovered that he had just recently started studying Bible doctrines and prophecies with his brother who belonged to a local church.)

How anyone could believe this escaped me. Of course, I had never read the Book myself, so my opinion could have been nothing more than a preconceived idea picked up from childhood and encouraged by Eastern philosophy. Nevertheless, I felt quite adamant about my stance.

"Do you really believe that?" I demanded.

Mark kept his cool, but mildly rebuked my lack of faith in his Book. At his gentle reproof, my mouth spewed forth a stream of profanity, and then to emphasize my exasperation, I stomped off into the night.

Shortly after my irrational display of emotion, I began feeling remorseful, so I headed back toward the house—but Mark had retired for the night. On the door I found a note. It said simply, "Mary, I think it would be best if we stay off of religious subjects for a while. Mark." My heart sank, and I lamented my own foolishness as I realized that I had just shut the door to any further discussions with him about the most important thing in my life—my spiritual quest.

During the next few days Mark made himself scarce. I felt lonely and hurt at the demise of our friendship and longed to apologize for my hasty words, but I just couldn't seem to find the right time.

Our conversation about the Bible plagued me. The more I thought about it, the more I realized that my negative feelings toward the Book were groundless because I had never taken the time to explore its pages thoughtfully. I remembered those special times of peace when my Catholic friend would read scriptures to me, and then I thought back to the instance when I had randomly turned to the love chapter in 1 Corinthians. Finally I concluded that I was being too narrow-minded.

One evening I lay tossing and turning on my bed. Mark and I hadn't spoken in days, and I missed my new friend terribly. I heard him stirring in the other room, and, secretly hoping that he might join me, I went out on the porch to gaze at the stars and get a breath of fresh air.

To my surprise and joy, Mark followed me out just a few minutes later. Bible in hand, he sat down beside me just as if we had never disagreed. Mark said nothing about our former argument, but simply began sharing some Bible texts with me that he had recently been studying.

This time I was receptive. If this Book was truly God's, then I wanted to know.

He and I revived our friendship and began studying the Bible together on a regular basis. Mark shared several religious books from his brother's church on the subject of Bible prophecy, and we began an in-depth exploration of Daniel and Revelation, two of the Bible's most prophetic books.

As we studied the prophecies within the Bible, its prophetic accuracy amazed me. The more I delved into Daniel and Revelation, the more I became convinced that this work was indeed more than human. The evidence in favor of the Bible's divine origin became stronger all of the time.

Still, I had my doubts, and I prayed that God might reveal the truth to me about these writings. Should I accept the Bible as truth or not? Should I put my wholehearted trust in it or not? Then one morning an experience took place that I dare label now as supernatural.

I awoke to what sounded like some sort of music, although the sound was fuzzy and indistinguishable. As I lay on my bed listening, a clear voice broke through with "MFSB—where the truth can be found." The letters particularly drew my attention because my initials at that time were MFS, and the phrase "where the truth can be found" intrigued me. The fuzzy music faded away, and I wondered at the mysterious voice and strange message.

Later that day I asked Mark if he had been playing his stereo in the morning. He answered negatively. That puzzled me all the more—for where else could the music have come from? (Our apartments shared a common wall, and at times I could hear his radio playing.) I didn't tell him what I had heard, thinking that maybe the voice was only a crazy dream.

Mark and I took one of our long walks that afternoon,

and on the way home I suddenly felt a great desire to look through his record albums and listen to some music with him on his stereo. After arriving back at our apartment house, I began flipping through Mark's wide selection of records attempting to find one to match my mood, but none of my usual favorites interested me. When I had almost run out of choices, I saw an album that I had never noticed before, and I gasped in astonishment as I read the initials "MFSB" printed boldly on the front cover.

"What group is this?" I asked Mark incredulously.

"Oh, that's Mother, Father, Sister, Brother," he replied nonchalantly. I had never heard of the group in my life.

Remembering the strange voice that morning, I grabbed the album and hurriedly opened it. To my further amazement, inside the cover were several scriptures out of Revelation—the very book in the Bible that we had been studying.

Nearly bursting with excitement, I told Mark of the early-morning voice that had audibly stated "MFSB—where the truth can be found." The conviction gripped us both that God had just used a supernatural experience to encourage me in the truth of His Word. It was as if He had led me on a little treasure hunt to find another clue in my search.

Soon afterward I had an intense dream in which I found myself standing in the midst of the universe with my hand stretched out as if to hold on to something. I felt a deep impression that the most important truths of the universe could fit into just the palm of my hand. Though in my dream I wondered how this could be, when I awoke the answer was clear—by placing the Holy Bible in it.

That evening, as Mark and I gazed upon the stars and wondered at God's magnificence, I told him of my dream. I also shared with him that now, because of our Bible studies, I was ready to accept Scripture as truth and as God's revelation to man. It was a moment of awesome significance as I received the Bible as my guide to truth and my communication from heaven. Mark rejoiced with me in my discovery.

He and I continued studying the Bible together, but now a new question started bothering me. If the Bible contained truth, then who was Jesus? Was He just another prophet, or was He something more? My inborn prejudices against Christianity still told me that anyone believing in Jesus as God must be less than intelligent. Still, because Jesus Christ was the central character of the Bible, I figured I should find out more about Him and how He might relate to my life. Again, I began praying fervently that I might know the truth about Him.

On my twenty-second birthday I found myself walking the streets of Ann Arbor and pondering the fact that I had no one to share my birthday with. My brother had not contacted me yet, my parents' card was late, and Mark had no way of knowing the date of my birth, so it appeared that for the first time in my life, my birthday would pass by unnoticed.

When I returned to my room I was surprised to find a brand-new book sitting on my pillow. I wondered if Mark could have somehow known my birth date and bought me a gift. After surveying the title, *The Desire of Ages,* and realizing that the book was a biography of Jesus Christ, I opened the front cover and read the inscription: "Mary, May God Bless You. Mark." At the top of the page, Mark had recorded the date, "August 12, 1976," but made no mention of a happy birthday wish. (I later confirmed the fact that he had no idea it was my birthday.)

As I skimmed through the pages, suddenly a delightful thought popped into my mind. Yes, there was someone who remembered my birthday after all—God! I thought that, perhaps, the book was His special way of telling me that He thinks of me even when it appears no one else does.

As I started reading the preface of the book, a spirit of love and sweetness filled the air, and the words deeply stirred me.

"In the hearts of all mankind . . . there are inexpressible longings for something they do not now possess. This longing is implanted in the very constitution of man by a merciful God, that man may not be satisfied with his present conditions or attainments, whether bad, or good, or better. . . .

"It is the purpose of this book to set forth Jesus Christ as the One in whom every longing may be satisfied . . . to help the reader to come to Him face to face, heart to heart, and find in Him, even as did the disciples of old, Jesus the Mighty One, who saves 'to the uttermost,' and transforms to His own divine image all those who come unto God by Him."[2]

The conviction that Jesus Christ is real and that in fact He is God took hold of me for the first time in my life. I knew, in that moment, that He was the one for whom I had been seaching so long. Though I couldn't prove it, the evidence of God's Spirit moving upon my heart was too strong to ignore.

During the next few days, though my heart still echoed the same sentiments, I rebelled at the thought of becoming a Christian. Somewhere in my background I had conceived the idea that Christianity is only for poor people, desperate people, unintelligent people. I may have been poor and at times desperate, but I didn't think of myself as unintelligent, and I certainly didn't want to label myself so by becoming a Christian. A commitment to Christ simply went against the grain, and my inward struggle at this time was tremendous.

Some days the conflict within me became so great that I could find relief only by going to the little brick church where I had first set eyes on that beautiful portrait of Jesus. Here I would kneel in front of the painting and gaze upon His face as peace flooded my soul. All too soon, however, I would have to leave, and the turmoil would envelop me once again.

The more I prayed, studied the life of Christ, and reviewed the events in my life since the beginning of my quest for love and truth, the more I felt convinced that Jesus Christ was my answer. The Bible, in which my faith was now unshakable, referred to Him as "the bread of life" (John 6:35), "the light of the world" (John 8:12), "living water" (John 4:10), "the true vine" (John 15:1), and my favorite of all, "the good shepherd" (John 10:11). Jesus said of Himself, "I proceeded forth and came from God." "I and my Father are one." *The Desire of Ages* describes Him in the following words: "His tender compassion fell with a touch of healing upon weary and troubled hearts. Even amid the turbulence of angry enemies He was surrounded by an atmosphere of peace. The beauty of His countenance, the loveliness of His character, above all, the love expressed in look and tone, drew to Him all who were not hardened in unbelief."[3] And I believed that my two special Bible-believing friends, Mary and Mark, had not happened into my life by mere coincidence, but, instead, had been sent by God in answer to my prayers for guidance. Now all that was left for me to do was to make a final decision and invite Jesus Christ into my life—but still I hesitated.

One evening, as I was walking and talking with Mark (who had just recently committed his life to Christ), he suddenly interrupted our conversation and pointed to a piece of paper under a tree. "I wonder what that is?" he said curiously—and I wondered why, in the midst of such an interesting conversation, he would be interested in a piece of trash. He walked over, picked up the paper, scanned it, and then handed it to me. "This is for you, Mary," he said, his eyes gleaming.

I looked at it in amazement. On the cover of the small

leaflet stood an ostrich with its head buried in the ground. Under the ostrich was a pointed question: "Could this be you? Are you delaying an urgent decision to accept Christ into your heart by burying your head in the sand when the evidence is all around you?" The tract ended with the admonishment: "Don't wait a moment longer. Accept Jesus Christ today."

The appropriateness of the tract was astonishing, and the fact that Mark noticed it lying under a tree was even more so. He grabbed me by the arm and exclaimed, "He's calling you, Mary!" I answered, "Yes, I know."

During the next few days I reviewed the past nine months, pondering once again the mysterious dreams and coincidences, my friendships with Mark and Mary, the studies in Bible prophecy, the deep stirrings I felt within as I studied the life of Christ, and the peace that I experienced as I gazed upon His portrait. I knew the time for decision was now or never, and I sincerely believed that God was calling me to a new life in Christ.

As I lay on my bed one evening, I made my surrender. "Jesus," I whispered, "if You are really there, and I believe You are, then please come into my heart tonight. I accept You as my God, my Saviour." I repeated the prayer over and over again as if to make sure that He heard me and believed me. No bolt of lightning hit me and no fireworks went off in my spirit, yet I knew that I had reached a tremendous turning point in my life.

8

LONG DRESSES AND HIGH-NECK COLLARS

"The effort to earn salvation by one's own works inevitably leads men to pile up human exactions. . . . All this turns the mind away from God to self."[1]

At the time of my decision to become a Christian, I did not fully grasp Jesus Christ's free gift of salvation[2] nor His role in my life as Saviour, Lord, and best friend. Oh, I may have understood the terms intellectually. I may have even been able to give a long discourse to somebody about them. But the truth was, I had only a small glimpse of God's wonderful love.

Because of this, I did not fully experience the peace and assurance that many Christians do when they first invite Jesus Christ into their hearts (although I did experience the joy of forgiveness and a relief from inexplicable guilt feelings that had plagued me all of my life). Instead, I simply knew for a surety that God had led me to Christ and that this was the direction I was to follow. My real heartfelt conversion into Christianity came only after a long and grueling experience with legalistic religion.

It began just three weeks after I accepted Christ when I joined a small Christian community tucked away in the woods and organized by a self-supporting group of the same denomination to which Mark's brother belonged. Mark had suggested that it might be good for me to get away from my old life and make a brand-new start. I wholeheartedly agreed, and when his brother suggested the old-fashioned community nestled amid acres and acres of beautiful pine trees, I jumped at the idea.

The community supported themselves with a growing natural foods business and took in anyone who was willing to work and share the group's lifestyle. Various family units housed young single people from all walks of life seeking a better way of life. They quickly accepted me as a new member.

The religious beliefs of the group were quite fundamental, and this I appreciated. The various doctrines espoused by the denomination from which the group originated inspired me, for they made such practical and spiritual sense and seemed to pave the way for a beautiful Christian life. Such beliefs as healthful living, Sabbath observance, and preparation for the second coming of Christ stood out. Agreeing with the doctrines, I felt glad to join a people of like belief. But from the first day I arrived, I sensed something seriously wrong with the spirit of the place.

I noticed that many women, along with their ankle-length dresses, Army boots, and high-neck collars, wore anxious expressions much of the time. The men, along with wrinkled shirts, baggy pants, and suspenders, donned serious faces more often than not. This is not to say that there existed no smiles, hugs, and genuine Christian love for one another—only that some unidentifiable tension in the air overshadowed them.

My first breakfast consisted mainly of boiled vegetables and zwieback, and as I partook of the meager fare I felt proudly pious to be entering into such a strict lifestyle in order to be saved.[3] At night, when I discovered that the community served only two meals a day (unfortunately I had eaten a light lunch to save room for dinner), I again took it in stride as another requirement for my right standing before God.

While I didn't mind the sparing lifestyle, the tension in the air did make me feel uncomfortable. I believed, however, that some important lessons awaited me, and I knew that the country atmosphere was beneficial, so after a few abandoned attempts to hitchhike away, I made a firm decision to stick it out for a while.

At the time of my arrival the community was in the midst of a marathon canning season. I found myself peeling peach after peach and washing jar after jar, sometimes beginning as early as 4:00 A.M. As I worked side by side with the other women, I became more and more convinced that something was terribly wrong in the community.

Mothers were expected to work half a day and to bring their toddlers with them. This caused a lot of undue stress that became evident in the mothers' attitude toward their children. One woman with an amputated right leg scrubbed floors—even though it often brought her unnecessary pain. Though we tried to sing our cares away, our strained smiles revealed the effect of a constant emphasis on work.

No one could leave the premises without special permission for fear of contamination with the outside world. I can vividly recall the day when my "homehead" tried to gain permission from her husband to take a few girls shopping for some personal supplies. The husband became visibly perturbed and only after much persuasion did he allow us to go.

Morning worships were a family affair, with everyone expected to be in attendance at six-thirty sharp, even if they were toting along small children. Often I thoroughly enjoyed the Bible presentations, but I noticed a definite inconsistency between the heartwarming Christian concepts presented and the spiritual condition of the community. Some sort of suffocating darkness hovered over the place, and few people seemed genuinely happy.

Despite my observations and premonitions that a great problem existed in the community, I became heavily involved in it. For a time I even believed that the place had a corner on the "truth," as we called it, and that to leave might be to "lose my salvation."[4] I was proud that I belonged to such a "spiritually superior" religious group and especially that I kept so many principles that other Christians didn't adhere to.

Totally enmeshed in the attitudes and teachings of the community, I began to see my standing with God as completely dependent upon my perfect obedience.[5] Of course, this caused quite a few struggles in my mind as I tried to understand what perfect obedience called for. Should I wear my skirt just a few inches below the knee or at midcalf? Was I sinning if I ate a snack in the evening? Must I wear my hair in a bun in order to please God? The questions were endless.

This belief also caused me to have a particularly critical attitude toward others, especially those of my new denomination who did not live in our community. If a woman visited our place in an outfit that I deemed immodest, I condemned her in my mind and prided myself in my own righteousness. At one point I actually believed that God couldn't save women who wore pants. Little did I realize how sorrowful my attitude toward others must have made God.

Our leaders regularly admonished us to share our faith with others outside our community, but I felt little ambition to do so. I wondered who on earth would want to go through what I was enduring in order to become a Christian. The burden of trying to become righteous was a heavy one, and besides the occasional bursts of pride I felt at having discovered "the truth," I was experiencing little real joy in my Christian walk. I can specifically remember one worship service when we discussed the meaning of the word *gospel.* As I discovered that it meant "good news," I thought to myself, I wonder why.

With my good friend Mark I had found the Lord Jesus.

But now legalism began clouding my true understanding of Christ. Webster's dictionary defines legalism as "strict, literal, or excessive conformity . . . to a religious or moral code." "Excessive conformity" perfectly describes the way in which our community carried out the principles of Christianity.

One young man (according to his friends) worried about how many almonds he ate in a meal. Although he was already beginning to look like a skeleton, he stood up during worship service one morning and asked God to give him "victory over appetite." Later, after moving to another community similar to ours, he wasted away and died of pneumonia.

A mother confided in me that her baby had been suffering from malnutrition because of their strict eating habits until a visiting nurse happened by and warned her of the infant's dangerous condition. She feared what might have resulted had not the nurse dropped in unexpectedly.

The community focused much attention on men-women relationships. The first week of my stay I was reprimanded for accidentally sitting next to a married man during morning worship. Men and women could not speak to each other unless it concerned business, and courtship procedures were closely controlled. To my dismay, I discovered that the strict principles between men and women affected not only single people but married people as well when a young wife tearfully told me that her husband no longer believed in "hugging" her.

The community did not overlook even the most minute details in life in its quest for perfect obedience. Because counsel was given that all parts of the body should be equally clothed, one woman considered tediously altering her underclothes in order to meet the regulation. Another man fixed up his study desk in an eccentric manner so as to meet the prescribed standards for posture perfectly.

The restrictive atmosphere allowed little individuality. At times I felt as if we were all robots living out the beliefs of the leaders without the freedom to think for ourselves. One day I heard a young teenage girl singing with the full joy of Christian love. Then, quite promptly, I heard another voice—harsh and loveless—reprimanding her for her loud vocal expression. To me it seemed the perfect analogy for the entire community—the sweet spirit of Christ being crushed out by a harsh, heavy hand of legalism.

The problem in the community, as I discovered later, was an obsession with outward reform without inner transformation. Jesus once said, "Woe unto you, Pharisees! for ye tithe mint, and rue, and all manner of herbs, and pass over judgment and the love of God: these ought ye to have done, and not leave the other undone" (Luke 11:42). The principles of right living that the community upheld were correct in themselves, but an overly strict adherence was taking precedence over such greater truths as love and mercy. (Case in point: The man who so carefully fixed up his desk was later convicted of manslaughter for severely beating a teenager as a method of discipline, and thus contributing to his death from pulmonary edema.) And without an emphasis on them, few real heart conversions were taking place.

Also, the focus on perfection caused most of us to concentrate on our faults and imperfections rather than on the glorious life of Christ. Our selfish preoccupation inhibited us from receiving the strength, love, and inspiration that we so needed in order to reflect Christ's character of love truly.

It was odd, but I saw so many similarities to the Eastern meditation group of which I had been a part that at times I wondered if I didn't belong to another cult. The measurement of spirituality by outward signs, the lack of real heart changes, and the strong peer pressure within the community alarmed me, but I continued to feel that I should stay. (Later on in my Christian experience I was grateful for the ability to explain the vivid contrast between true Christianity and legalism because of my heavy involvement with the latter.)

Despite the dark atmosphere in the community, I managed to enjoy the natural surroundings and found worship services enriching. The hard work was good for me, the plain food a boon to my health, and the strict association principles a helpful precaution for my romance-prone heart. My new life was beginning, but I yearned to see an example of true Christlikeness to refresh my soul and assure me that I was on the right track. Like a breath of fresh air that example arrived one day—all the way from California, my home State.

9

A CHRISTLIKE EXAMPLE

*"There is an eloquence far more powerful than the eloquence of words in the quiet, consistent life of a pure, true Christian."**

"Did you know that a young man just arrived from California?" a friend of mine asked as we attacked huge mountains of Sunday afternoon dishes.

"No," I said curiously. "What part of California?"

"I think they said Redlands," she answered.

"Redlands!" I exclaimed. "That's where I'm from."

I could hardly believe that someone all the way from my hometown had just arrived to live in our community. Although speaking to a young man privately was against the rules, I decided to sneak up beside him the first chance I had and ask if he really was from Redlands.

That afternoon I saw our newcomer strolling down the pathway toward our eating hall. After taking stock of his six-foot-two-inch stance, wavy brown hair, and friendly smile, I gathered up my courage and casually approached him.

"Excuse me," I said shyly, "I was told that you're from Redlands, California—is that true?"

"No," he answered cheerfully, "I'm from Redding, and that's in the northern part of the State."

I remarked that my informer must have mistaken Redding for Redlands, and then I expressed my delight that a fellow Californian had arrived. After our brief exchange I walked hurriedly on, not wanting to endure another embarrassing reprimand for getting close to a male.

Immediately I noticed his easygoing attitude and relaxed manner in contrast with the tension that I perceived in other community members. His sunny demeanor was uplifting, and I felt enriched to have spoken with him.

The more I observed Kent (I was supposed to call him Brother Wuestefeld, but I could never get the hang of pronouncing his last name), the more his spirit of love and acceptance for all he came in contact with impressed me. He didn't seem so wrapped up in the rigorous rules and regulations, although he adhered to most of them quite willingly. Instead I perceived that his spiritual experience was centered in a genuine love for God and a desire to serve Him with all his heart.

To my delight we ended up working together in the natural foods factory—I as a secretary and Kent as a factory worker. In this situation we were able to speak with each other daily and sometimes even share a little bit about our lives. Thus a special friendship began to develop between us.

His consistent Christian life inspired me to seek a deeper relationship with God. Kent didn't preach, he didn't lecture, and he didn't criticize those who did things different from the way he did. He simply accepted people as they were and exhibited an honest love for God and for his fellowman. This, I often thought, was the kind of religion that I longed for, but unfortunately I still found myself caught in the trappings of legalism.

Kent's friendship was refreshing amid the heavy atmosphere of legalistic Christianity, and his kindness often lifted my spirits just when I needed it most. Inwardly I hoped that someday we might pursue our friendship on a deeper level, but I knew that the time for that had not yet come. I kept my dreams to myself, content to enjoy a casual relationship with him.

10

HOME AGAIN

*"Only by love is love awakened."**

Three months after joining the Christian community I secured permission from the leaders to go home for Christmas, and eagerly boarded a jetliner for California. I arrived home piled high with religious tracts, health foods, and a determination to teach my family about God. As it turned out (although I didn't realize it until much later in my Christian experience), they were the ones to teach me.

Fourteen months earlier my parents had seen me dressed in casual pants, drinking cocktails and espousing women's lib. Now I came bursting into their lives dressed in nineteenth-century clothes, eating health foods, and preaching religion. Despite the drastic turnabout in my life, they accepted me with open arms and mouths closed to criticism. Unfortunately, I was the one on the critical end.

It is a strange phenomenon that the ones who preach "freedom of thought" the loudest when they are breaking out of a family or societal mold often push their ideas the strongest once they have found what they are looking for. Recently I read that even Martin Luther, the great leader of the Reformation, fell into such a trap in his later days. I must admit that after I arrived home for Christmas vacation I displayed this paradox also.

Expecting everyone to immediately see things the way I saw them, I preached health reform and gave books about Jesus to my family and friends for Christmas. Again my family accepted my actions in love and never once reprimanded me for being overzealous in my newfound faith. They even listened politely. As I look back now, the patience they exercised seems incredible.

My father was kind enough to take me to church every week, and my mother went shopping with me despite my strange attire and embarrassing habit of handing out religious tracts to the store clerks. As odd as I must have seemed, we managed to have a wonderful visit, and I cherished every day at home. The freedom that I experienced was a welcome relief from the oppressive atmosphere that I had just left. Though my parents did not profess Christianity, they exhibited one of God's greatest attributes—that of unconditional love. Years later, as I reminisced about the visit, I learned a valuable lesson concerning God's true character from the genuine love demonstrated by my family.

Fortunately, somewhere around this time I had a dream that greatly enhanced my attitude toward my family. It was so vivid and awe-inspiring that I shall never forget it.

As the dream unfolded, I found myself in the hallway of my parents' home. Inside the bedroom I could see my mother lying on the bed in a deep sleep. I seemed to be pondering how I could awaken my mother to the truths of Christianity.

Suddenly an overwhelmingly beautiful Presence filled the house. I knew instantly that Jesus Christ had just entered. The peace I felt in my heart and the total fulfillment that I experienced was incredible. Then Jesus spoke to me: "Just tell your mother you love her. Tell her with all your heart."

As I walked into the bedroom and looked at her, a profound love filled my soul. I bent over her still form and whispered, "I love you," but those simple words could hardly convey the abundance of love that I felt for her at that moment.

My mother began to stir. Then my dream ended. But the message came through loud and clear—only by love can love be awakened.

As I awoke from my dream, I felt deeply convicted that my tendency to appear dogmatic and critical must be replaced with the love of Christ, and that my sole duty toward my family was to love each member as Christ does. I can honestly say that since the time of my dream (although I'm sure I've failed many times in manifesting God's perfect love) my family and I have shared a beautiful and open relationship with one another as we seek to convey our strong affection—and to accept one another just as we are.

Christmas vacation passed all too quickly, and although I treasured the time with my family, I knew I had to head back toward my new home in the chilly Midwest. Many of life's lessons lay yet unlearned, and I believed that my place was with the little community of struggling Christians. So, after three wonderful weeks in sunny California, I winged my way eastward once again.

11

GROWING

*"The plants and flowers grow not by their own care or anxiety or effort, but by receiving that which God has furnished to minister to their life."**

Shortly before my Christmas vacation a terrible tragedy had taken place in the community to which I now returned. The death of a young man served to awaken community members to the twisted theology and oppressive atmosphere in which we were all living and to initiate some much needed changes.

The drama began one crisp fall morning when a community administrator announced that we had "lost one of our brothers." He went on to explain that a teenage member of our community had died of a severe flu. Needless to say, the news shook those of us who already sensed a dark and foreboding atmosphere within the place. It seemd odd that someone would succumb to the flu without seeing a doctor or going to the hospital first.

The next few days I overheard women whispering and praying together, asking for God's mercy on our community. It made me all the more suspicious, and I wondered what the real story behind the teenager's death could be. Then I heard someone mention the word "beatings."

Soon more information began trickling in, and I learned that the young man, a former drug addict with severe emotional problems, had received a severe beating as a means of discipline. Apparently, the same administrator who had announced his death had secured from the parents permission to spank and had then himself meted out the punishment.

When the coroner came to examine the young man's body, he discovered severe bruises and swelling all over the lower torso. The evidence seemed strong enough to connect the beatings with the boy's sudden death, and the authorities brought charges of manslaughter against the one who had administered the "discipline." (Later found guilty of manslaughter, the defendant was sentenced to several years in prison.)

Meanwhile, our community fell into shock. At first many tried to justify the beatings by reasoning that such action may have helped the young man to "give his heart to Jesus" and "be saved." Some talked of "persecution" from the "outside" (meaning unfair treatment from the sheriff's department), and one young woman even referred to the jailed administrator as "our hero."

But gradually we all began to realize that the severe beatings only pointed to our twisted theology and obsession with obedience. Leaders in sister institutions called for an entire revamping of our administration, and shortly after I returned from Christmas vacation, a brand-new governing board began operation. Slowly but surely, a new day was dawning.

With new leaders at the helm, the atmosphere gradually became happier and more relaxed. Some of the woman began shortening their skirts and letting their hair down to look more modern. Meals became tastier as our menu included more fresh fruits and vegetables. Husbands and wives actually began strolling together arm in arm, and news of forthcoming babies brought smiles to us all.

Though I still suffered from serious misconceptions about God's love because of the heavy legalistic indoctrination I had experienced, I too began growing in Christian understanding and maturity. The more I allowed God into my life through prayer, Bible study, and fellowship, the more my Christian experience flourished.

For instance, Christian terminology and doctrines that had been cloudy in my mind now came into focus. Terms like *sin, Saviour,* and *salvation,* which had always annoyed me in my non-Christian days and somewhat confused me during my first few months as a Christian, now took on tremendous meaning. I saw sin not merely as a set of do's and don'ts set up by some church, but as those actions and attitudes that keep us from furthering our understanding of God and from loving the way He does. Because I discovered more and more sin in my heart as I studied God's great principles of love in the Bible, I felt ever more convinced of my need for a Saviour—one who could free me from my selfishness and restore me to God's image of love. As I accepted Christ's forgiveness for my past and present sins and believed in His power to re-create me, I truly found my Saviour—and my promise of salvation (or the deliverance from the power and effects of sin and the hope of eternal life).

Appreciation for the little things in life, such as a warm bed, friendship, and good food began to grow in my heart also. For so many years I had received these things as though owed to me. But now, under the somewhat sparse conditions in our community, just a simple thing as a warm shower after trudging home from work in the Michigan winter brought joy and gratefulness to my heart.

For the first time in my life I began to understand the important relationship between our practical lives and our spiritual lives. In the past I had the mistaken idea that our spirituality was separate from and above the everyday humdrum routine. So what if I neglected my homework, carried forty extra pounds of weight, and often displayed impatience under the slightest provocation? As long as I exercised my "spirituality" by contemplating the existence of God, I was superior to the common person who cared only about "material things."

This myth exploded, however, as I realized that God cares about the material as well as the spiritual and has given us many practical instructions in His Word concerning our everyday lives. Furthermore, I saw that the quality of our spiritual lives mirrors itself in the quality of our practical lives, and that we cannot separate the two. For instance, God's principles of hard work (Proverbs 12:11), proper care of our bodies (1 Corinthians 3:16, 17), and self-control (Galatians 5:22) will manifest themselves in the meeting of appointments, a healthy body, and a sweet temperament. In other words, the more we become like God, the more we will reflect His qualities in our everyday lives.

Perhaps the most important growth during this time took place in my understanding of Jesus Christ. For the first several weeks of my new life as a Christian I retained some doubts toward His divinity and superiority over other great religious leaders. But the more I became acquainted with Him through His Word, the more I appreciated the uniqueness of His message.

I came to the conclusion that Jesus could not have been just another "good man" who walked the earth. He was either the greatest liar who ever lived or God incarnate. He clearly declared His eternal existence ("Before Abraham was, I AM" [John 8:58]), His Messiahship (John 4:26), and His ability to give eternal life (John 11:25). Not only did He teach principles of right living, but He offered an entirely new nature through oneness with Himself (John 3:1-21) and claimed the power to forgive sins (Matthew 9:6). And while other "prophets" and "good men" lie silently in the grave, Jesus Christ is yet alive (John 2:19; Acts 10:40, 41), still offering mankind "the way, the truth and the life" (John 14:6).

In view of the historical fact that Jesus, in only three and a half years of ministry, ignited a theological revolution that has caused untold numbers of men and women to take their stand for love and truth, I could hardly believe He was a great liar. Instead, I became more and more convinced that He is just who the Bible says He is—"God with us," the Saviour of mankind (Matthew 1:22, 23).

Even though I was growing, my wrong concepts of religion stunted my ability to perceive God's love and experience His peace fully. I still believed that my acceptance by Him and my assurance of eternal life centered upon my perfect obedience, and I still carried the heavy burden of seeking my own righteousness. My false concept often discouraged me and continued to spawn a critical attitude toward others, especially fellow Christians. I longed for the kind of Christianity that emanated from my friend Kent. His constant cheerfulness and dependable smile revealed a free and happy relationship with God.

When Kent moved about an hour away to work at one of our community's health food stores (the community owned and operated several natural food stores and restaurants across the country), I felt quite disappointed. Fortunately, I still saw him on the weekend, and as always, our conversations were refreshing.

At times I felt a deep need to share my heart and soul with another human being, and I wished that it could be Kent, but that seemed an impossibility. First of all, he gave no indication of any romantic interest toward me. Second, he was quite musical, and I could hardly carry a tune. And last but not least, he was thin and I was plump. I pictured him marrying a svelte soprano, and I hardly filled the bill. But I continued to treasure his friendship, secretly hoping that God might someday bring us together despite our differences.

Another year passed by quickly. I continued to study, pray, fellowship, and, by God's grace, to grow. My constant prayer was that God might reveal Himself more fully in my life.

Once more I flew home for Christmas and had a lovely time. When I returned to the community, however, I found that most of my good friends had transferred to various restaurants, and a wave of extreme loneliness hit me. On top of it all, Kent had moved even farther away to a restaurant in Wisconsin, and I could no longer count on his encouragement to give me a lift. In my loneliness and longing for human companionship, I became hopelessly entangled with one of our new community members and fell heartfirst into another infatuation.

12

INFATUATED

"The man [or woman] who is bound in the chains of . . . infatuation is too often deaf to the voice of reason and conscience; neither argument nor entreaty can lead him [or her] to see the folly of his [or her] course."[1]

I don't remember the first time I met him—I don't even recall our first conversation together. All I know is that shortly after Christmas break I found myself in the exhilarating yet relentless grip of infatuation.

Stan was about my height with thick black hair and an attractive European accent. He appeared deeply spiritual and quite sincere in his search for a meaningful relationship with God. Since men and women were allowed to fellowship more freely in our community now, it didn't take long for Stan and me to strike up a friendship.

A recovering alcoholic, Stan was just days off the bottle. My friends tried to warn me that he was not stable enough to pursue a serious relationship, but I just couldn't resist the temptation to share my deepest thoughts with him and to hope for a blossoming love. Soon Stan's eyes revealed that he too had succumbed to the emotion.

A few weeks into our relationship, we acknowledged our feelings of love for one another. Though we weren't supposed to be alone, we managed to pass notes and to sneak in private conversations when no one was looking. Our attempts at discretion proved unsuccessful, however, and soon several community leaders advised us to break off our relationship before it turned into an ill-advised marriage.

I resented those in the community who tried to "run my life," and I attributed their questioning of our relationship to an out-of-date philosophy of male-female relationships. Now that romantic love was just within my grasp, I resisted anyone who might try to snatch it away from me.

The more I became acquainted with Stan, the more I recognized areas of insecurity and instability in his character, but my feelings blinded me to the dangers involved in marrying a man not yet grounded in life. I could not heed the advice that more experienced Christians were trying to offer, but instead viewed marriage as a cure-all for both his and my problems. (Only later in life did I look back and realize the appropriateness of the counsel we were receiving, and the dangerous path on which we were treading.)

Stan and I began to criticize the leadership for clinging to narrow views and old-fashioned ideas. Despite urgent warnings to prayerfully reexamine our relationship, we stubbornly forged ahead. Just five weeks after meeting, we were considering marriage and making plans to leave the community.

As Stan and I became more serious about our plans to depart, we decided to pray together and ask for God's blessing and guidance. Since meeting him, I sensed that my relationship with God had been slipping, and now I longed for some evidence that He approved of our course. But as we sent our supplications to heaven, I felt only an anxious stirring within, and the usual peace I found in prayer escaped me. Some quiet voice seemed to be pricking my conscience and warning me of danger—but the grip of infatuation was too strong and I chose to ignore it.

My situation could not have fit the following description better: "Two persons become acquainted; they are infatuated with each other, and their whole attention is absorbed. Reason is blinded, and judgment is overthrown. They will not submit to any advice. . . . Like some epidemic, or contagion, that must run its course is the infatuation that possesses them; and there seems to be no such thing as putting a stop to it."[2]

Stan and I made tentative arrangements to fly out to California and stay with my family for a while. The community leaders voiced their dismay when we announced our decision, but I didn't care—I was determined to find the happiness that I "deserved." When one of the leaders asked, however, if we would be willing to separate for the rest of the evening and spend the night in meditation and prayer, I could hardly refuse. After all, since I claimed to desire God's will for my life, I should at least be willing to present our plans to the Lord one more time. Heeding the advice, Stan and I retired to our respective rooms.

A thousand thoughts began flooding my mind as I lay down on my bed to review the last few weeks. I remembered the quiet voice that had so often admonished me, telling me that Stan and I weren't ready for marriage. I recalled the anxious forebodings that I felt every time he and I knelt down to pray. I thought of the multitude of counsel that I had received warning me about his instability as manifested in his recent bout with alcoholism. And I began to feel more and more uncertain about our marriage plans.

Then Kent's face came before me, and I thought of his strength of character, his unwavering Christian commitment, and his balanced Christian life. My secret dreams that someday I might be his wife flashed through my mind. A strange conviction gripped me that Kent was to be my husband and not Stan, even though Kent was hundreds of miles away and had never shown any romantic interest.

Despair and confusion swept over my soul. Kneeling by my bed, I began pouring out my heart to God. Although I realized that I was being stubborn, the prayer "Thy will be done" seemed so hard to come by. I feared that the fluttery feelings, emotional high, and dreams of marriage would all vanish if I let go of Stan.

Little did I know that several community members had gathered together during this time to pray for me also. Those whom I had resented so much were now lifting their hearts up to heaven in supplication that I might see the danger ahead and that I might surrender my heart entirely to God. A great spiritual battle raged in my soul, and they had gathered in my behalf.

After wrestling in prayer most of the night, I finally succeeded in sincerely but feebly uttering the words "Thy will be done." I knew that by surrendering my will, I was giving God permission to work His will in this situation, and I sensed His Spirit moving in a mighty way. Resting uneasily on my bed, I waited for morning to bring God's answer.

A few hours after placing my relationship with Stan into God's hands, I heard a knock at the door. As I opened it, I faced Stan and tried to read his expression. What had he discovered during his evening of prayer? Would he still want to go through with our plans to leave?

Smiling weakly, he told me of his decision. He explained that during the night he had become convinced of our need to be apart for a while, so he had decided to leave that very morning—without me. He still professed to care for me, but now said that he felt uncertain about our plans to get married. After suggesting that we continue to pray about our relationship, he hurried off to pack his belongings.

Emptiness and heartache immediately swept over me. I thought back to my prayer only a few hours earlier and felt certain that it was God's answer to my petitions—but for a moment, I didn't want to accept it. Even as I started questioning His purposes in my fresh heartbreak, however, that quiet voice that had so often admonished me now whispered words of assurance and peace.

As soon as Stan left the community, a strange thing happened. I literally felt as though a strong hand had relaxed its grip on me. A sense of freedom that I had not known for weeks came over me, and I rejoiced even in my sadness.

Later on in the day, standing by my desk at work, Kent's face flashed into my mind once again. A second strong conviction seized me that he was to be my future husband. For a moment I thought the impression might only be my hopelessly sentimental imagination, but because it was so strong and forceful I felt sure that it must have some significance.

The following weeks were not as painful as I expected. It seemed as though God was administering some kind of emotional anesthetic as He removed Stan from my heart. Soon he and I both concluded that our relationship was not meant to be, and Stan moved permanently to another Christian community.

Months later I heard that Stan's unstable character had manifested itself more fully through the use of drugs and the involvement in some strange religious doctrines. As time passed, it became more and more obvious that our union would have been disastrous. So often we think that God is trying to deprive us of pleasure and satisfaction when He is really attempting to spare us great pain and heartache. Hindsight illustrated this to be the case in my relationship with Stan. I will ever be grateful for my praying friends, concerned leaders, and heavenly Father, who through their combined efforts helped me to escape such a serious error in emotions and judgment.

As I share this experience, hundreds and thousands are suffering from the pain and frustration of mismatched marriages. Many times I have witnessed the cycle of headstrong infatuation, ill-advised marriage, broken dreams, and then divorce. Only by God's grace did I narrowly escape such a trap myself. The key was in surrendering my will—just in the nick of time—to an all-knowing, all-wise God who had my best interests in mind.

I believe that if we could implement three Biblical principles in every relationship, we might avert hundreds of bad marriages. These principles are prayer (James 1:5), counsel from godly friends and/or parents (Proverbs 24:6; Exodus 20:12), and abstinence from heavy physical involvement before marriage (1 Corinthians 6:18). By seeking God's will daily and being willing to listen to His voice, by asking at least three or four trusted friends, counselors, and/or parents for advice, and by steering clear of the gripping influence of premarital sex, many aspiring young Christians might escape marital disaster.

An experienced mother and Christian counselor once advised: "Great care should be taken by Christian youth in the formation of friendships and the choice of companions. . . . Weigh every sentiment, and watch every development of character in the one with whom you think to link your life destiny. The step you are about to take is one of the most important in your life, and should not be taken hastily. While you may love, do not love blindly."[3]

Looking back now, I can see that God certainly knew what He was doing by removing Stan from my life. For, by marrying him, I would have missed out on one of the most wonderful surprises of my life. (More about that later.)

13

BATTLE WITH BULIMIA

"Jesus loves to have us come to Him just as we are, sinful, helpless, dependent. We may come with all our weakness, our folly, our sinfulness, and fall at His feet in penitence. It is His glory to encircle us in the arms of His love, and to bind up our wounds, to cleanse us from all impurity."[1]

Just as my struggle with infatuation was ending, another battle emerged. It was not a new one, but a powerful resurgence of a problem originating in my college days. Six years ago I didn't know it had a name, but today the medical world would label my predicament as bulimia.

Webster's defines bulimia as "an abnormal and constant craving for food." It is often accompanied by the unpleasant compulsion to get rid of excess food in the stomach by the old finger-in-the-throat trick. In bulimia, food becomes the emotional comforter for every type of problem, and its victims usually consume large quantities of food at one sitting.

My compulsive eating began fairly early in life, but didn't develop into full-scale bulimia until college, after the traumatic event of separating from my fiancé. By the end of my sophomore year, I found myself hiding food, sneaking food, and snitching food (from my roommates). I could down an entire pound of graham crackers in one meal, and my weight climbed to 185 pounds. Although I tried myriads of diets, losing a few pounds here and there, I found nothing to cure my overeating.

It is difficult to explain the power that food can have over a person unless one has experienced it himself, but let me illustrate further. Often I would whip up a batch of muffins in the middle of the night and eat all of them before they were even baked. If, by chance, my muffin ingredients were low, I would pedal my bicycle to the nearest all-night supermarket and buy some other treat (preferably doughnuts). When neither option was available, my roommates' food supply became the target of my craving—much to my embarrassment the morning after. (I'll never forget the humiliation I experienced when a roommate of mine discovered a gooey mess of peanut butter, raisins, and honey in her raisin container—the remnants of a strange concoction that I had whipped up the night before.)

Bulimia is much like alcoholism, smoking, or drug dependency in that a person is deeply emotionally and/or physically dependent on a substance taken into the body. All these problems are extremely difficult to overcome, and bulimia is no exception.

After I left college and became a Christian, my problem with bulimia subsided for a while. But shortly after Stan and I separated, it sneaked up on me and waged a fierce attack. (Most likely the emotional upheaval experienced during my bout with infatuation triggered the latest bout with compulsive eating.)

Because I had vowed never to let bulimia gain control of me again, I couldn't believe it was back. And in view of my new conviction that our physical health has an intimate connection with our spiritual well-being, I felt worse than ever about my dilemma. I tried desperately to beat the monster back, but its grip on me seemed to get tighter all the time.

I began praying fervently about my struggle, but often no sooner had I prayed than I would rise and repeat my gluttonous actions all over again. Time and time again I found myself hiding in kitchens and basements, devouring whatever I could come up with (there wasn't that much to choose from in our community) and feeling guiltier by the minute. Never before had I felt such utter helplessness, and such a need of God's power in my life.

One day, as I was strolling down the road soaking in some spring sunshine, I knelt by an old oak tree and began pouring out my problems to God. As I prayed, a Scripture verse came forcefully into my mind: "If we confess our sins, he is faithful and just to forgive us our sins, and to cleanse us from all unrighteousness" (1 John 1:9). As I contemplated the words, I felt as though God was speaking directly to me.

The words "cleanse us from all unrighteousness" deeply impressed me. Suddenly I saw that God was promising to cleanse me—not just by covering me with His righteousness, but by actually freeing me from my life-controlling problem. In the past when contemplating the passage, I had always noticed the forgiveness aspect but overlooked the cleansing action. Now I felt the wonderful assurance that God, with my cooperation, would give me victory. I arose from prayer with a heart full of faith and a deep inner conviction that I was not fighting my battle alone.

The weeks that followed brought little relief, yet still I clung to God's promise of cleansing. Although I saw little evidence, I believed that somehow, someway, God was working on my behalf.

One morning during church service I grew restless and slipped out quietly, seeking some place to pray and meditate alone. I settled myself by a blooming flower garden and, after letting the irises, pansies, and daffodils cheer my heart, bowed my head once more to seek my Saviour.

The morning was particularly bright and beautiful. I told God of my helplessness and pleaded for His special power, adding that I would do anything or go anywhere if He would only help me overcome my battle with bulimia once and for all. Placing my life in His hands, I said, "Lord, this is Your battle. I'm willing to cooperate with You the best I can, but I know I can't win it by myself. You've got to fight this battle for me."

Once again I experienced the deep assurance of God's love and concern for my life. As I continued to pray, my desperation dissolved, and by the time I was finished my heart felt light and full of faith. It seemed as though for the first time I had fully released my struggle and left it in God's hands. Now I knew in the deepest crevices of my soul that when I did finally gain victory over the gripping compulsion, all of the credit would go to God. Words like *willpower* and *self-control,* which I so often threw at other struggling individuals, seemed to crumble in the dust, and I began staking everything on God's power alone.

It was good that God let me come to this point. So often during my life I had belittled others in the midst of their struggles and prided myself that I was not so "weak." But as I came face to face with my own helplessness during my battle with bulimia, I began to experience a new compassion and understanding for other people. I realized that each and every human life is a varied mixture of strengths and weaknesses, of achievements and failures, and that none of us can esteem ourselves greater than another (Philippians 2:3). We are all equal in God's sight, and He offers to accept each one of us where we are, whether it be in the White House or on skid row. He then promises to begin restoring us into His perfect image of love. God is no respecter of persons, and neither should we be. He used my problem of bulimia to break down my heartless pride and replace it with a new acceptance of my fellowman.

A few days after completely surrendering my struggle with bulimia to God, I received a summons to the house of the director of our community. He was aware of my desire to get a new start somewhere, although I don't think he knew why. (My problem was too embarrassing at that time to share with anyone.) I felt that a change in my surroundings might help me to get an edge on my dilemma, so I was planning to speak to him about moving to a Christian community in New Hampshire that taught printing skills—an aspect of journalism that had always interested me. To my complete surprise, the director had another destination in mind.

"Mary," he said with conviction, "I think the restaurant work would be good for you. You can develop your cooking and cleaning skills and prepare yourself for marriage."

Marriage, I thought to myself. I've just about given up on that. "Where do you want to send me?" I asked curiously.

"Well, Madison, Wisconsin, needs some help. Why don't you pray about it, and we'll discuss it more later."

I couldn't believe my ears. My good friend Kent had gone to Madison. Could it be possible that I might soon be working with him once again? It seemed too good to be true. And then, again, it scared me. I just didn't feel ready for another heartbreak, and I knew that if I were to live in close contact with Kent, I'd probably fall head over heels for him. How could I be sure, or even hope, that he would feel the same about me?

I started praying that God would direct my future plans in a special way, asking Him to close the doors on the Madison idea if such a move was not His will. If heartbreak awaited me, I honestly did not want to be near Kent. I remembered my impresssions that Kent and I would be husband and wife someday, and I felt that perhaps this new direction in my life was truly within God's providence. But I left the matter in the hands of God and the leadership, perfectly willing to go wherever they chose to send me.

The day came when our community board met to make decisions about personnel. Outside thunder and lightning raged, and inside I felt an awesome impression that a most important decision concerning my future was in the making. I thought about my ongoing struggle with bulimia and my prayers for deliverance. At the same time I contemplated my special friendship with Kent and my hopes for a deeper relationship. And as I meditated on both areas of my life, I distinctly sensed that the decision would be God's answer to my needs.

Shortly after the meeting ended, the director called me up to his home once again. "Mary," he said with a smile on his face, "can you be ready to leave for Madison by tomorrow morning?"

"Why, sure," I answered as my heart leaped for joy. It would be good to have a change, and it would be great to see Kent. As I ran home to pack my things, I knew deep inside that the decision to leave for Madison was not only mine and the leadership's but God's, too.

That evening I took another serious look at my problem with bulimia. Once again I vowed that with God's help—and I knew it could be only with His help—I would put it out of my life forever. I promised the Lord that I would do everything I could to leave the problem behind, and I asked Him for His special strength.

Late the next afternoon we arrived at an old farmhouse in a little town outside Madison. Here I would reside along with several other young women and two houseparents. The apartment next door housed all the young men—including Kent.

When Kent and I saw each other the next morning at our community breakfast, he didn't seem overly excited, but was friendly as usual. But my heart was thrilled to be near my special friend once agian.

As the days of restaurant work unfolded, I could see

the wonderful wisdom and mercy of God in leading me to Madison. For the first time in several months I started gaining control over my eating habits. We all worked late into the evening, and I didn't even have a chance to binge. The house in which I slept had no refrigerator, so midnight raids on the icebox became impossible. (I must admit, however, that I did lie awake several times thinking about what goodies I could confiscate from the freezer in the garage next door—fortunately, I never had the nerve to try.) I knew without a doubt that God had purposely placed me in the best environment possible for battling my problem, and I felt so grateful for His gracious love and direction in my life.

At times when temptation did begin to overpower me, I called on God for strength to overcome—and almost invariably He delivered me. Each victory helped me to establish new habits and surmount old ones, and the edge over my foe grew greater all the time.

The change in my circumstances, the warm fellowship with my new circle of friends, and God's special power in my life all helped me to lick the worst manifestations of bulimia. However, I continued to maintain a heavy figure. Though I no longer gorged myself with all sorts of sweets, I wasn't cutting down on calories enough to lose weight. One day a painful comment brought this fact vividly to my attention and gave me greater zeal than ever to gain complete victory.

The remark took place while a group of us were gathering firewood for the winter. When our director, who was visiting for the weekend, saw a big pile of brush that needed to be crushed down, he called out, "Hey, where's Mary? She'd do a great job of stomping on this." To add to my humiliation, Kent was standing somewhere nearby. The comment devastated me. Disappearing into the woods by myself, I once again called upon my Lord.

"God," I said desperately, "when am I finally going to

overcome this problem of mine completely? You've helped me to get over the worst part, but I'm still fat. Please help me once and for all." Again, I knew the key to victory lay in God's power, and I arose believing that help was on the way.

About two weeks after I prayed for complete victory, I noticed my appetite lessening. Small amounts of food now seemed to satisfy me, whereas previously I would wolf down at least two platefuls in a meal and top that off with a dessert. Slowly but surely I began losing weight. Though I had struggled and struggled for years to reduce, now it seemed almost effortless. By the time Christmas vacation rolled around again, about twelve extra pounds had melted off.

This time when I went home for Christmas I didn't feel so tempted to gorge on chocolate and cookies as in the past. (The first two Christmases at home as a Christian I found myself devouring large chunks of chocolate during the night in complete contradiction to the health principles that I so adamantly espoused.) My appetite remained small, and I continued to lose weight. It was wonderful, incredible, and too good to be true . . . but it was true. For the first time in years I was regaining my shapely figure. Six and a half years have now passed since my bulimia disappeared, and I can honestly say that I have never struggled with the condition since that time. By God's grace I have maintained a slim figure, and with little effort at that.

Some might try to explain my victory over bulimia with some biological or psychological theory, but I firmly believe that it was God who delivered me from my terrible compulsion. And I believe that the same God who so graciously helped me can deliver anyone from anything no matter how long he or she has been possessed by it.

The key is to confess our need, believe that God will cleanse us of our problem, and then cooperate with Him as He uses circumstances, people, and His power to carry out the transformation. We may feel that we have no control over a particular temptation, but if we acknowledge our helplessness, spread out our case before the Lord, and follow His leading, we can be assured of His victory. As one religious writer has said: "You cannot change your heart, you cannot of yourself give to God its affections; but you can *choose* to serve Him. You can give Him your will; He will then work in you to will and to do according to His good pleasure."[2]

The victory may not come instantly. Often we must struggle in His strength against inherited and cultivated tendencies for days, months, or even years until new thought patterns take precedence over old ones. It is true that sanctification is a process "of a lifetime"[3] and that we will be continually growing.

In extreme cases, however, where years and years of indulgence have deeply ingrained habits, God may sometimes choose to intervene supernaturally and impart instant deliverance. I have heard story after story from alcoholics, smokers, and others in which the particular indulgence has disappeared from the life in a moment or a day through God's special mediation. In my case God allowed me to struggle for a time and then, near the end of the battle, intervened in a special way to free me completely.

The miracle that God performed in my behalf put a new testimony of His love and power in my heart. I rejoiced at the experience through which I had come even though it had involved so much pain and frustration, because now I could share a personal story of deliverance with others. I looked forward to the future with anticipation and wonder at what God would do next in my life.

14

SONGS OF LOVE

"He has given me a new song to sing, of praises to our God" (Psalm 40:3, T.L.B.).

About the same time that God began conquering my bulimia battle, He also began working in another area of my life. What He did next came as a completely unexpected yet much appreciated surprise.

It all started one evening while I was visiting in the home of a couple who often came to our restaurant. As we sat chatting, I spied an oddly shaped stringed instrument sitting in the corner. Noticing my curiosity, the husband identified it as a lute and asked if I'd like to take it home and learn how to play it. Remembering my futile attempt in the past to learn the guitar, I declined.

Later on that evening the man again inquired if I'd like to take the lute with me. It seemed odd that he should be so insistent, but finally I complied. I figured that it would at least give me something to talk with Kent about, considering his musical interests and abilities and his talent on the guitar.

The next day I asked Kent to teach me some simple chords on the lute. My fingers didn't seem as clumsy this time around, and before long I had mastered three or four chords and learned a little finger picking.

About a week after acquiring the lute, I composed a simple song entitled "I Sought the Lord," describing my conversion experience. A few days later I shared it with the couple who had lent me the instrument. To my surprise, they loved it and enthusiastically encouraged me to keep up my creative efforts. I exchanged their lute for a used guitar that they also happened to own, and in a matter of days new chords and new songs started coming together for me. Something special was happening in my life.

One morning, when all the restaurant workers had gathered for worship, the leader asked me to sing a composition I called "Only by Love." In it I portrayed the compassionate methods of healing and teaching Jesus displayed during His ministry on earth. My knees shook along with my voice, for I wasn't used to performing in public, but I managed to eek it out anyway. At the end I heard some faint amens, but that was about all. Embarrassed, I wondered why I had ever attempted to share it in the first place.

Later on during the day, however, Kent commented that my song had really "touched his heart." I was happy that it had meant something to somebody, especially since that somebody was him. I secretly wished that he might sing harmony for it and help me to arrange it on the guitar. It wasn't long before my wish came true.

I don't remember exactly how it happened, but soon Kent added his masterful guitar playing and beautiful tenor voice to my simple song and made it come alive. Surprisingly, we found that our voices blended quite well (somehow I had finally acquired the ability to carry a tune), so we began practicing and singing together quite often. Needless to say, my heart burst with joy.

As this musical miracle began to unfold in my life, I felt more and more convinced that God was preparing me to become Kent's wife. I believed that my rapid acquirement of musical skills and the gift of songwriting could be no mere coincidence. So often I had despaired that I did not share Kent's musical interests and feared that he would choose a life companion far more melodious. But now the gap had been bridged, and I hoped that a deeper relationship with my special friend might be just around the corner. Still, Kent indicated only platonic interest in me.

He and I began singing together occasionally at small churches in the area. I enjoyed standing beside him, sharing our music with others. As I continued to learn more chords and to write more songs, Kent helped me as much as he could. All too soon Christmas vacation came, and we parted for our respective homes in northern and southern California.

Coincidentally, my brother was serving a medical internship in the same county where Kent's parents lived. Kent suggested that I give him a call if I happened to be in that area. It sounded like a great idea to me, and when I visited my brother's place for a few days, I dialed Kent's number immediately.

To my great disappointment, he didn't sound happy to hear from me at all. My overeagerness probably made him cautious. Although we did arrange to go to church together, the unfriendly tone of his voice gave me the jitters, and I canceled at the last minute, telling him that I had come down with the stomach flu.

What began as a case of nerves turned into a physical and emotional disaster, and my excuse of the stomach flu was no exaggeration. By midmorning waves of rejection and nausea rolled over me, leaving me buried in despair. I started fearing that all my hopes concerning Kent were mere illusions conjured up by a sentimental heart. The haunting tone of his voice combined with my dizziness and aching bones soon enveloped me in darkness.

In the midst of it all, I picked up my Bible to glean some ray of hope for myself. Barely able to realize God's presence, I found a scripture that helped me to visualize His love: " 'Fear not, for I have redeemed you; I have called you by your name; You are Mine' " (Isaiah 43:1, N.K.J.V.). I clung to the verse and repeated it again and again in my mind.

Then I found a most inspiring passage in a favorite book of mine entitled *The Ministry of Healing*. It read like this: "Many who profess to be Christ's followers have an anxious, troubled heart because they are afraid to trust themselves with God. They do not make a complete surrender to Him. . . . Unless they do make this surrender they cannot find peace. . . . Our heavenly Father has a thousand ways to provide for us of which we know nothing. Those who accept the one principle of making the service of God supreme will find perplexities vanish and a plain path before their feet."*

Though for two days I struggled with nausea and depression, these words helped me to see light beyond the darkness. I clung by faith to the promises of God even though I felt that my hopes and dreams about Kent had been a mirage.

As I recovered from the flu and returned to the cheery atmosphere of my parents' home, my depression lifted considerably and I was able to enjoy the remainder of the Christmas holiday thoroughly. I still feared that I had been mistaken about a future relationship with Kent, but I was determined to trust God no matter what happened.

Soon I headed back toward snow-covered Wisconsin and my job at the restaurant. When Kent and I met face to face once again, he continued to act aloof, and I became more convinced than ever that he was trying to avoid me. I tried to interest him in some new songs that I had written, but my efforts seemed in vain.

During this painful time I did some real soul searching. I realized that I had wrapped up too many of my hopes and dreams in Kent rather than in God's provision for me. One sentence continued to echo in my mind—"Unless they do make this surrender they cannot find peace." Once again I struggled to yield my entire life to God and to leave my plans in His hands. Finally I confided in a friend one evening that I had given my dreams to God and was trusting fully in Him—despite my great disappointment in Kent's apparent disinterest.

A few days later I noticed Kent doing a lot of counseling with our visiting director. Usually in our community young men did that before entering into a "courtship"—or an official dating relationship with the girl of their choice. I strongly suspected that this was the case with Kent—and now I was really hurt. Yes, I had surrendered my dreams to the Lord, but was I ready for Kent's interest in another woman? Perhaps, I thought, this was precisely what God had been preparing me for during the past few weeks. And then one morning as I walked up the restaurant steps after praying for God's grace and guidance, I received the greatest surprise of my life.

15

THE DESIRE OF MY HEART

"Delight yourself also in the Lord, and He shall give you the desires of your heart" (Psalm 37:4, N.K.J.V.).

As I entered the restaurant, I almost bumped into the director's daughter who was working with us for a time. She caught my arm and whispered, "I have some news for you."

My interest in Kent was no secret to Julie. And because she was the director's daughter, I figured that she might have some inside information concerning Kent's counseling sessions with her father. She motioned toward the basement stairs, and we hurried down together.

I feared that the moment of truth had arrived. Was she about to confirm my suspicion about his interest in another girl? Could I bear to hear this news? By the time we settled on the basement carpet my hands felt cold and clammy and my heart pounded nervously.

Looking at my friend questioningly, I braced myself, expecting a wave of emotional pain to hit me any second. Solemnly, Julie said, "Kent's interested in someone."

My heart fell. "Who?" I asked agonizingly, not really wanting to know.

Trying to keep a straight face, but then breaking out into a gigantic grin, she exclaimed, "You!"

I couldn't believe my ears. "Me?" I asked over and over again as I threw a big bear hug around her. "Are you sure? Are you absolutely sure?"

As Julie confirmed her information, my heart

soared—although Kent's recent aloofness toward me made it hard to believe. I could only think that perhaps he had been exercising special caution in our relationship as he considered the serious matter of further involvement. He was not one to make rash moves, and as I discovered later, he had been contemplating this one quite carefully.

In our community we observed an old-fashioned dating system called "courting." When I first learned of it, I scoffed, thinking it incredibly outdated. But as time went on in my Christian experience, I learned to appreciate the principles involved more and more.

In proper "courtship" procedure, a man first takes time to pray seriously about the woman of his choice and then to counsel with trusted friends and/or parents about the possible relationship. If, after meditating and counseling, he feels confident of his choice, he approaches the woman and asks her to "court." The term *court* means to date on a steady basis and to become acquainted in such a way as to determine whether or not the two of them should pursue marriage.

According to Julie, Kent was about ready to pop the question, having satisfied himself through prayer and counsel that he desired to seek a deeper relationship with me. It brought me incredible joy, enhanced by the inner conviction that God was leading us together.

Now I wondered how he would approach me. I waited one day, then two days, then three. Nothing. I asked Julie again, "Are you sure he wants to court me?" She reaffirmed her original information. I could hardly stand the suspense.

Finally, one morning Kent rode to work with the early crew (of which I was a member) instead of coming in a few hours later as usual. That particular day we arrived together with a little extra time to spare, and I knew our special moment had come.

After we had scurried downstairs to put our coats and

boots away, I noticed him lingering in the basement longer than usual. I decided to make things a little easier on him by remaining also. He sat nervously on a table swinging his legs while I sat in a chair about six feet away, fingering my guitar strings.

Kent fidgeted with something and then turned toward me. "Mary," he said seriously, "there's something I have to talk to you about."

"Oh?" I replied feigning ignorance. "What's that?"

"Well, I've been praying about it, and I'd like to ask you to court."

"Oh, I'd love to," I smiled.

"Really?" he said with amazement. (He probably wondered why I seemed so calm. If I hadn't learned of his interest beforehand, I most certainly would have collapsed in shock.) "That was easy," he mused, and then a big grin broke out on his face also.

We talked for a few more minutes about God's leading and our mutual desire to spend time together, then headed upstairs to begin the day's work. I felt tremendous joy that now we would be sharing our lives, our thoughts, our hopes, and our dreams, and I looked forward with great anticipation to the beautiful new adventure of a relationship with Kent.

The days of courting were wonderful yet somewhat insecure. Because of my past experience I kept fearing that once again my dreams might all shatter. But Kent was strong and sure of our involvement, reminding me always of God's hand in our relationship and assuring me that in Him our growing love would hold fast. Instead of things going great for a while and then fizzling out, Kent and I just kept getting closer all the time. The wonder of experiencing a genuine, caring relationship with a sincere young Christian man gradually began to build new confidence within me.

When I asked Kent why he had given me the cold

shoulder during and after Christmas vacation, he confirmed my suspicions about his attitude of caution. He explained that he didn't want to get my hopes up by manifesting special interest in me until he had determined his course of action. He also confided that there was a bit of shyness involved, too.

Then he shared with me the fact that during the previous fall, while reading a chapter on marriage, he had felt deeply impressed that I was to be his future wife. Because he had no romantic interest in me at that time, he paid little attention to the thought until it struck him again a few weeks later as he was getting ready for bed. After the two experiences, he began contemplating the possibility of becoming involved on a deeper level.

Kent leveled with me that although he had always treasured our friendship, the extra weight I carried had bothered him. Amazingly enough, the impressions about marrying me came just before I started losing weight. So even though I was still plump when he felt inspired to consider courtship, a few months later I had slimmed down considerably. When I returned after Christmas break Kent saw me as a new person, and his romantic interest blossomed.

It was truly amazing to see how God had prepared me for Kent by investing me with musical talents and giving me a brand-new figure. As I contemplated the situation, I knew beyond a shadow of a doubt that God had been leading us together since the first day we met.

Getting to know Kent was a great boon to my spiritual life, just as I suspected it would be. The love and devotion that he manifested toward God inspired me tremendously and gave me spiritual strength. I shared all my struggles with him concerning my understanding of salvation, and I told him of my fears that I could never be saved. He tried to assure me that my hope of salvation had its basis solely on a faith relationship with Jesus

Christ—but it took years for me to grasp that beautiful fact.

One evening as we were attending a prayer meeting, the light of salvation by faith alone broke through my confusion for a moment at least. In the midst of our pastor's discourse, he looked at us solemnly and asked, "How many of you here know that if you died tonight you would be saved eternally?" A few people meekly raised their hands, but I honestly did not know.

"Why," he continued enthusiastically, "we can all know that we have salvation right now if we are in a relationship with Jesus! Our salvation is in Him!"

The idea that I could be assured of a place in heaven without first attaining perfection was a relatively new thought to me. Up until that moment the possibility of eternal life seemed like a very iffy matter. If I did enough things right, if I lived up to the light that I knew, and if my good works outweighed my bad in the judgment, then I might be saved—but I really couldn't count on it.

As we drove home, I discussed the subject with Kent once again. For a fleeting moment a beautiful breakthrough occurred in my relationship with Christ as I threw away the heavy burden of works and trusted fully in my partnership with God for the promise of salvation. Unfortunately, it lasted only a few days, and soon I fell back into confusion. I couldn't understand how I could trust Christ with my salvation when I had so much work to do! I still thought that I had to be perfect in order to merit a home in heaven. It took almost five years before the revelation I received that night would completely penetrate the layers of past misunderstandings and fill my heart with a glorious new freedom in God.

Kent and I walked together, read together, prayed together, and worked together. We found much comfort and joy in each other's company. Soon we were making plans for marriage, both felt convinced that our lives were meant to become one.

June brought our wedding day, more glorious than we could have ever dreamed. God gave us a perfectly clear sky, the fragrance of pine, and colorful summer flowers to adorn our outdoor wedding. As His Spirit drew near, our hearts overflowed with joy and thankfulness. In front of family, friends, and our Father in heaven, Kent and I vowed our love and finally became husband and wife.

16

HARD LESSONS TO LEARN

"You cannot exert an influence that will transform others until your own heart has been humbled and refined and made tender by the grace of Christ."[1]

Shortly after we nibbled the last crumbs of our pineapple whole-wheat wedding cake and said Goodbye to friends and family, we sped off in our new van (a gift from my parents) toward northern Wisconsin for a two-week camping trip. We basked in the sun, wrote songs together, and enjoyed the beautiful scenery. As wonderful as our honeymoon was, however, I discovered that my love for Kent was not perfect—at least by the Bible's definition. While the Scriptures define love as patient, kind, and unselfish (1 Corinthians 13:4), I often exhibited moody and selfish characteristics.

Despite my shortcomings, Kent continued to reassure me of his love and to cope quite well with my various moods. Daily I thank God for giving me a husband who loves me regardless of my unpredictable temperament. Kent's faithfulness and devotion helped me to realize God's unconditional love more fully as time went by.

Not only did I realize that my love for Kent needed maturing, but shortly after we were married, I became painfully aware that my love for others was sorely lacking. It all began when Kent and I decided to launch out on our own from the restaurant work and pursue a career in selling Christian publications.[2]

Included in Kent's new job description as a literature evangelist (one who sells Christian literature door-to-door in order to share the gospel of Jesus Christ) was the opportunity to conduct Bible studies with anyone indicating an interest. Not only did I accompany my husband door-to-door, but I also took on the challenge of giving Bible studies to various customers. I thought that I was ready to evangelize the world, but like Moses when he slew the Egyptian (Exodus 2:12), I discovered that I was not yet ready for such an advanced task.

After a few months I began to notice that our Bible study interests responded much better to Kent than to me. His gentle approach did not always acquire sales, but it did win friends—whereas my more zealous attitude occasionally seemed to offend. When someone disagreed with me doctrinally, I deemed it my duty to prove and press my point. I justified my dogmatic attitude by telling myself that if an individual didn't have the truth, then he couldn't be "saved." My understanding of a Christian's salvation still rested much more on the particular doctrines he believed than on his relationship with Christ.

My motives weren't all bad, but they weren't all good, either. I honestly did want to introduce others to the God who had done so much for me since my conversion to Christianity, and I really did want others to experience the joy of forgiveness and the hope of deliverance that I myself had experienced. But though I wouldn't admit it to myself, interwoven with my sincere desire to share God's love was a selfish aspiration to bring lots of people into our church so that others might notice my "superior" evangelistic ability and my "commendable" dedication to God. Apparently my self-worth was still wrapped up in my ability to achieve rather than in my love relationship with Jesus.

Needless to say, the Bible studies that I gave personally, apart from my husband, didn't accomplish much. Not one individual found a lasting relationship with God during this time. Frustration and disappointment welled up inside me as I considered my inability to witness effectively—and then I remembered my dream about the pure drop of love.

Just as in the dream, I was trying desperately to spread love, but failing miserably at my task. However, the dream had not ended in failure, but with a profound piece of heavenly advice, and as I recalled the admonition to drink of the love myself, I suddenly realized why my efforts at evangelism were all coming to naught. Although I had discovered God's love, believed in it, and even tasted of it, I had not yet begun to drink of His love deeply enough so as to manifest His magnetic qualities of meekness, humility, and compassion.

"He who would confess Christ must have Christ abiding in him. He cannot communicate that which he has not received. The disciples might speak fluently on doctrines, they might repeat the words of Christ Himself; but unless they possessed Christlike meekness and love, they were not confessing Him. A spirit contrary to the spirit of Christ would deny Him, whatever the profession."[3]

One day a painful confrontation with two close friends confirmed my suspicions about myself. In essence, God performed what I like to call "open-heart surgery" on me. Although it hurt terribly at the time, as the wounds healed, my heart began functioning far better.

The knife fell one evening while Kent and I visited Steve and Barbara, two special friends who were searching for a deeper experience with God. Many a night we had spent together sharing personal experiences and discussing religious beliefs. Over a course of time a strong bond of friendship had developed.

Because Steve and Barbara were living together—but not married—I felt a strong desire to see them "tie the knot." I also held high hopes that one day they might become members of our church. Unfortunately, I had developed a critical attitude toward Steve, because in my estimation he was impeding the progress of his partner.

That particular evening I chose to give them a piece of my mind, all "in love," of course. I challenged them on their religious beliefs, and then suggested that perhaps their relationship was interfering with their personal growth. My comments may have been sincere, and may have even been spoken in a calm, loving manner, but when I criticized their relationship I was stepping on forbidden ground. Although they said nothing at the time, I soon discovered that I had deeply hurt them.

About a week after our conversation Steve called my husband and asked him to come over to his home for a private conference. When Kent arrived, both Steve and Barbara expressed their reaction of hurt and anger over my latest verbal onslaught and then accused me of having a self-righteous attitude in other incidents also. According to a note that they sent home for me, I came across like an Indian trying to get scalps rather than a Christian trying to lead others to God's kingdom.

When my husband shared their feelings with me, my first reaction was outrage. Emphatically I declared that I was in the right and that what I had said had been only for their benefit. I couldn't stomach the thought that my friends viewed me in such a horrible way, and for the first few days I blamed everything on them.

But as I began to pray about the situation, I had to admit the ugly truth. After much struggling, I finally admitted that their assessment of me was all too true. Steve and Barbara were not the first people whom I had offended with my air of superiority—and as for the scalps theory, I could actually recall looking about in church, counting the number of guests there that I had personally invited, and then puffing up with pride in my great "soul-winning" capability.

Finally I came face to face with the fact that my attempts to share God's love were failing because my motives did not come solely from a deep, unselfish desire to lead others to Christ. A censorious spirit, a self-righteous attitude, and an achievement-oriented motivation made me a failure at genuine soul winning. Up to this point in my Christian experience I had only tasted of God's love, but now I understood that to be successful in sharing His love I must begin drinking deeper and deeper drafts until it overflowed from my heart to others. But how?

As I pondered this problem, I realized that to drink from Christ's pure fountains one must first allow Him to empty the heart of the polluted waters of selfishness. Because my heart still contained so many un-Christlike attitudes, it had little room for His living springs of love. It became obvious to me that I was not yet ready to be involved in evangelism.

One day I knelt down and specifically asked God to give me an experience similar to that of Moses during his shepherding years. Moses, like myself, had determined to rescue his countrymen from bondage, only to discover, after slaying an Egyptian in a rash moment of self-righteousness, that he needed a much deeper understanding of God before he would prove successful. God, in His infinite mercy and wisdom, made Moses a shepherd in order to develop traits of patience, reverence, humility, and faith.[4] As in Moses' case, I too had wounded someone with my self-righteous attitude, and it became apparent that I also needed an experience to humble me, soften my heart, and draw me closer to God before I could successfully share God's love with my fellowman.

Sincerely I apologized to Steve and Barbara, although it did little to alleviate their hurt feelings. I learned the hard way that hasty words can lead to years of alienation.

Fortunately, as time went by, God's Spirit reconciled our hearts and we became good friends once again.

I continued to pray for a "shepherding" experience, and I felt sure that God was about to answer my prayer in a special way. He certainly knew better than anyone else how much I needed a change.

17

MY BUNDLE OF JOY

"The sympathy, forbearance, and love required in dealing with children would be a blessing in any household. . . . The presence of a child in a home sweetens and refines."[1]

Shortly after asking God for an experience to refine my character and enhance my ability to love, I noticed a strange taste in my mouth, the beginnings of nausea, and feelings of depression. One day I commented to my husband, "Either I'm going crazy or I'm pregnant."

From the beginning of our marriage we had allowed nature to take her course concerning babies, and for almost two years nothing had happened. I doubted that I might be pregnant now, but the strange symptoms told me something must be going on inside my body. After a few weeks of suspense, we decided to try a home pregnancy kit. To our great joy and surprise, the test results were positive.

My husband and I rejoiced in the news of a forthcoming baby—deeming my pregnancy a beautiful gift from God and an answer to my prayers. I felt certain that motherhood was just the experience I needed to develop His love within my heart. Soon, instead of trying to evangelize the world, I would be home with my baby, learning invaluable lessons in tenderness and compassion.

I continued to work with Kent in the book-selling business, but my various symptoms, such as nausea, made it more difficult than usual. Pounding on doors late into the evening just didn't suit me anymore. Fortunately, a job opened at our church's day-care center, and I jumped at the chance of getting some experience with children. After I talked with its director, I was hired immediately.

I found my work with little ones extremely rewarding. Their unpretentious smiles and sincere affection fed my soul. I didn't even mind changing umpteen diapers every day. Something about caring for children really hit the spot for me, and I experienced a satisfaction that I had not known in literature evangelism. While selling books, I noticed myself trying to manipulate and pressure, but now I could just love and be loved without any ulterior motives.

The more I dealt with children, the more I began anticipating the birth of my own child. I couldn't wait to hold a baby in my arms that was all mine. Finally, on January 13, 1982, Daniel Alan Wuestefeld arrived.

That evening after Daniel's birth, I lay awake all night practically bursting with joy. God's presence filled my hospital room with the atmosphere of heaven, and it seemed as though angels rejoiced with me. In the morning, when they placed him in my arms, my adoration knew no bounds. The love I felt for my son was deep and intense from the first moment we met.

I have heard that a mother's love for her child is perhaps the deepest form of human love on earth, but I never expected my heart to be flooded with such joyous emotions and tender feelings. And as my love for Daniel continued to increase, my understanding of God's love intensified also.

It is said that Enoch, whom God transported to heaven, never fully understood God's love for mankind until he fathered a son of his own. "As he felt the deep, yearning tenderness of his own heart for that firstborn son, he learned a precious lesson of the wonderful love of God."[2] That became my experience also. As I prayed over my baby while he lay innocently sleeping, as I felt motherly hopes and fears concerning his future well up inside my breast, and as my love grew stronger every day even in the midst of his naughtiness, I truly began to understand God's care and unconditional love for each one of us.

Becoming a mother not only provided me a new insight into God's character and enhanced my ability to view others with compassion, but also gave me new motives in life. Instead of a selfish desire to achieve in the area of soul winning so that I might impress others with my dedication to God, I began to know a deep longing to see my little boy become a Christian. As I looked into his sparkling blue eyes and felt that maternal love swell within my heart, I finally realized why Jesus died that He might save even one human being. For the first time in my life I understood the kind of love that made Christ want to take our rightful place on the cross. Any remaining desire to accomplish those "great achievements" in life now faded in the light of my growing ambition to lead my little child into the presence of Christ.

As the days of loving and caring for my precious son passed by, God continued His process of cleaning spiritual debris out of my heart with His all-powerful cleansing agent of love. Though much of the clutter still remained, He managed to clear enough pride and selfishness away to make room for a love that longs to reach out to others in genuine concern. I found myself praying that God might use me, not for my own glory, but as an instrument in His hands to heal aching hearts and fill empty lives with His love. As always, God heard my prayers and led me into an exciting experience with a young mother on the verge of divorce.

18

SHARING GOD'S WAY

"Search heaven and earth, and there is no truth revealed more powerful than that which is made manifest in works of mercy to those who need our sympathy and aid." *

Witnessing effectively for Christ involves a lot more than simply telling others of His beautiful plan for mankind's salvation—although obviously that is a vital ingredient. According to *Webster's*, the word *witness* means to "furnish proof of," and in order to be an effective witness for God, we must furnish proof of His love to the world by actively demonstrating it in tangible ways. Then and only then will the story of God's love become meaningful to our friends and families.

As I've mentioned previously, though many opportunities to share God's love had come my way since my conversion, I hadn't seen many lives changed as a result of my witnessing. Too many of my motives were selfish and too much of my professed love shallow. But after becoming a mother and developing a deeper capacity to love, God gave me my first fruit-bearing experience with a friend facing serious marital problems.

Debra, a mother of three and wife of a church official, had been a casual acquaintance of mine for several years. When I heard via the grapevine that she and her husband had separated, my sympathy immediately went out to her. Being a wife and mother myself, I could imagine what agony she must be facing, and when I learned that she was filing for divorce, I especially felt sorry for her children.

With a genuine longing to see Debra and her husband reconciled, I began praying that God might use me in some way. Fortunately I now understood that if we simply make ourselves available to the Lord for use rather than rashly applying our own solution to a problem, things will turn out much better in the long run. Only through His wisdom, love, and guidance can we ever make a difference in someone else's life.

One day I ran into Debra in the mothers' room at our church. We exchanged a few comments about our children, but I never once mentioned Debra's separation. Longing to let her know that I was genuinely concerned about her problems, I put my arm around her as we were leaving and whispered, "I just want you to know that I love you and that I'm praying for you." She smiled at me, but didn't seem too impressed by my words.

That afternoon the phrase "I love you" kept echoing in my mind. Was it just an empty cliché that I had uttered with no real action behind it? How could I make those three little words come alive for my friend? I remembered times past when I had spoken that same phrase with good intentions but never backed it up. This time, determined to underwrite my statement with action, I continued to pray that God might reveal a way for me to draw closer to Debra. Nothing I would say or do could have meaning unless I revealed my care and concern to her in a tangible way.

It wasn't long before I heard that Debra would be out of a baby-sitter soon. Right away I recognized my opportunity to befriend her, but part of me rebelled at the thought of three more little ones running around my small apartment. Keeping up with my rambunctious 2-year-old seemed hard enough, and I couldn't imagine a houseful of children under 5.

Immediately a struggle began within. On the one hand I saw baby-sitting as a perfect chance to develop a deeper friendship with Debra. Perhaps, I thought, by offering my services God might use me in some way to avert her pending divorce. On the other hand, I wondered if God really expected me to take three more children into my home. Wasn't this asking a bit too much? Couldn't I find some easier way to befriend Debra?

The controversy went on for several days. At times God's attributes of unselfishness and benevolence would triumph and I would surrender to the task. But more often than not, my own selfishness would be the victor.

One chilly November morning I ran into Debra at the supermarket. In the course of our conversation I asked if she had gotten a new baby-sitter yet. She looked at me hopefully. Her need reached past my many layers of selfishness, and I immediately offered my services. As soon as I told her of my decision, a wonderful peace came over me and I felt sure that I was making the right decision.

As time went on and I tackled the challenge of mothering Debra's three little ones, I discovered how important it is for love to come dressed in working clothes. Not only did my willingness to baby-sit for Debra break down barriers and establish a deep and special friendship, but it opened up many opportunities for me to talk seriously with her about the consequences of divorce.

This time I didn't preach to my friend—nor did I tell her what decisions she should make. I simply made myself available for conversation and counsel, and prayed that God would put the right words in my mouth at the proper time. There were moments when I wanted to say something, but the Lord impressed me to remain silent. Since then I've come to see how wise it was to keep still. There were also days when I felt afraid to speak, but the Lord prompted me to say something in love. Hindsight shows me God's wonderful leading in these instances also.

One day I felt particularly troubled about Debra's situation. Although I had no evidence to that effect, I sensed that she had reached a crisis point. I told my husband my fears, and we prayed for her around noon. She was due to pick up her children in a few hours, and I hoped to have a good talk with her then.

When Debra arrived, she appeared sullen and unapproachable. Feeling an urgent need to strike up a conversation, I asked her quite openly how things were going between her and her husband. She mumbled some sort of negative reply and began hurriedly gathering her children together. Again sensing a need to break through her defensive barrier, I commented that I believed there was still hope for her marriage. At that, she placed her children's coats on our table and sat back on the couch.

Suddenly, without warning, Debra burst into sobs. As I stared at her in surprise, she began confessing her faults and admitting that her husband was not the sole cause of her marital problems. Not knowing quite how to handle the situation, I simply put my arm around her, told her I loved her, and assured her of God's love also. After conversing a little more, we prayed together and asked God's Spirit to move on both her and her husband's heart in a special way.

After Debra left, I feared that I had not encouraged her as much as I might have in such a crucial moment. Perhaps I had even failed her. I could pray only that God would work mightily on behalf of my friend.

Then to my great delight and surprise, the phone rang about an hour later. In a cheerful and enthusiastic voice Debra explained that God had just convinced her to cancel her divorce—which would have been final in three days. Having had no idea that it was going through so soon, I marveled at God's mysterious promptings in my heart. That evening Debra and I celebrated her decision over dinner. She looked as if a two-ton load had lifted from her shoulders, and her eyes sparkled with new life. She spoke of her desire to seek God's will and to put her children and husband first. A few days later Debra told me that God had confirmed her decision to reunite with her husband by pointing out a special Scripture verse. Not only was her marriage being revived, but her desire to seek a deeper relationship with God was also growing. It was evident that Debra's life had taken a dramatic turn for the better.

The following week her husband wired her a dozen red roses, and Debra told me she was in seventh heaven. Tremendous joy filled my heart that they and their children would not have to experience the heartbreak of divorce.

Many times Debra expressed her gratitude to me for caring enough to reach out during her times of distress. But I could only thank God for allowing me to touch another human being with His love in a life-changing way. Finally, my dream of sharing God's love effectively was beginning to come true.

Through such experiences my husband and I have discovered six steps to effective witnessing. We call the formula "AFFECT." You can apply these guidelines to anyone (non-Christians and Christians alike) in need of some spiritual encouragement. The steps are as follows:

A—Accept the person just as he is.
F—Familiarize yourself with his needs.
F—Fulfill tangible needs as far as possible.
E—Explain what Christ has done for you when opportunity arises.
C—Continue to pray earnestly.
T—Trust God with results.

The initial step is a crucial one. To draw close to a person, we must first allow God to cleanse us of any critical attitudes within our hearts. Not only will a judgmental attitude inhibit us from loving unconditionally as God does and thus greatly weaken our ability to demonstrate His love, but it will also serve to drive people away as they pick up on our negative feelings. In order to gain another's confidence and friendship we must first love and accept them just the way they are.

After we have asked God to put His unconditional love in our hearts, then we must seek to familiarize ourselves with the needs of our friends by asking questions and showing genuine interest in their concerns, whether they be small or seemingly insurmountable.

Once we know a person's particular problems, it behooves us to do something about them. For instance, an elderly person might require help in fixing meals, a single mother might need the oil changed in her car, or a lonely teenager might just long for some time to talk. As we seek to fulfill these needs we will create an atmosphere of confidence and love.

During such times of service we should constantly be looking for opportunities to share what God means to us and how He has helped us and guided us throughout our lives. It is important to note that we should never act as another person's conscience by dictating his actions or beliefs. Instead, we should pray and seek for the right moment to speak. Our witness will be most effective if we focus on Christ's love and forgiveness rather than on the mistakes and/or misconceptions in our friend's life. (After all, we are not perfect either!)

Our efforts to share God's love will be absolutely fruitless if we do not pray ourselves. God is the only one who can change a life, and we must ask for His Spirit to move on the heart of our friend. We must never think that our efforts alone can accomplish lasting changes in a person's life.

And last, but certainly not least, we must trust God with the results. Our only responsibility in witnessing is to love and to share the best that we can. If we mistakenly feel that it is our duty to transform lives, then dogmatic attitudes may creep into our hearts. But as we realize that heart transformation is God's jurisdiction, we will remain free to love the way God does—with no strings attached.

19

HIS UNCONDITIONAL LOVE

"God gives, not as a means of control, but as a natural expression of His very nature."[1]

Shortly after my experience with Debra, another close friend of mine called with some more unsettling news. Linda, who only days earlier had expressed her growing appreciation of our church, now suddenly announced that she was leaving our denomination.

Changing churches may seem like a minor incident to many people, but the fact is, most religious groups are quite jealous for their membership. A church is like a giant family, and losing a family member hurts. Also, the beliefs that we hold so dear and deem so vital to our Christian faith are an integral part of the particular church we join, and when we see a close friend departing from the church family we often fear that they are straying from important doctrinal convictions. For these very reasons I felt saddened and hurt at my friend's decision to look for another church.

Linda explained that she no longer felt comfortable with our denomination because of some overly dogmatic attitudes which she found within the local congregation. She said that, after all, "it's love that really matters, not the denomination" and announced her decision to seek another Christian fellowship. After questioning her about the sudden change in sentiments, I discovered that her new fiancé was not happy with our church either.

As we talked, I sensed a wall rising between us—not because of any attitude on her part, but because of my own exclusivity. Although we did manage to end our conversation on a friendly note, I felt a certain coolness toward my friend where just hours ago there had been great warmth.

As I pondered my reaction the following morning, I realized with great dismay how easy it is to fall into the trap of accepting or rejecting our friends on the basis of their actions and/or beliefs. Although we use the word *love* so freely with our friends and families, we find ourselves harboring critical or unkind feelings when they do not see things exactly as we do.

This response of inwardly criticizing and discriminating against those who see things differently from the way we do has caused terrible results when carried to an extreme. Men and women possessing the courage to stand up for their inner convictions have been tortured and murdered while, to a lesser degree, thousands of individual thinkers have found themselves outcasts from their religious affiliation for choosing to view traditional issues in a new light. Marriages have broken up, friends have separated, and parents have even disowned their children because of differing beliefs. And so often such incidents occur in the name of truth.

Genuine truth, however, does not seek to force the conscience by threats of humiliation, pain, or abandonment. "It is Satan, and men actuated by his spirit, who seek to compel the conscience. Under a pretense of zeal for righteousness, men who are confederated with evil angels sometimes bring suffering upon their fellow men in order to convert them to their ideas of religion; but Christ is ever showing mercy, ever seeking to win by the revealing of His love."[2] God gently reminded me that to reject or belittle Linda in any way, even in the privacy of my own heart, would be to fail at loving her as a true friend.

Soon after our phone call I wrote Linda a long letter and poured out my thoughts concerning her decision to leave my church. To love someone unconditionally does not mean that we can never share our particular convictions, but it does mean that we must always present them in a loving, unobtrusive manner. This I tried to accomplish, and then at the end of my letter I reaffirmed our friendship and assured her that no matter what direction she chose, our relationship would remain secure.

As I mailed the letter, however, I wondered if I really meant what I had said. What if she permanently rejected the church that was so dear to me? What if she thoroughly discarded those doctrines that I held so sacred? Could I continue to accept her and to love her freely? Or would I harbor secret feelings of resentment and criticism? Silently I prayed that God would fill me with the kind of love for my friend that knows no denominational barriers.

It wasn't long before my written profession of unconditional friendship found itself put to the test. Linda announced via the telephone that she and her fiancé would be paying us a visit soon. While happy, I was also somewhat apprehensive. I hoped that our differences would not stand between us and that God's love would triumph in my heart. If I could not totally love and accept my friend just the way she was, then no matter what I professed, I really had no truth abiding in me. Genuine truth is rooted and centered in the all-encompassing, unconditional love of God.

Shortly after hearing that Linda and her fiancé were coming my way, I came across an impressive editorial. It spoke about our tendency to give in order to get. For instance, we give love in order to obtain a certain response. A Christian might offer kindnesses and encouragement in order to convert a person to Christianity. At first glance this doesn't sound so bad, but when these tendencies are examined at a deeper level we find hidden within a subtle desire to control.

The editorial went on to explain that we often perceive God's love in this way. We mistakenly think that God loves us in order to elicit something from us, such as our hearts, our time, or even our money, when in reality God loves us simply because it is His very nature to love. He gives, not to get, but as a natural expression of His character.

As I contemplated these thoughts, a deep conviction took hold of my conscience that the motive of getting still tainted too many of my own relationships. I could see that even in my friendship with Linda many of my words and actions contained subtle efforts to change her way of thinking to mine. Just recently I had been planning to shower her with special love when she came to visit in hopes that I might persuade her to change her mind about leaving our church. A statement in the editorial spoke directly to my heart about this: "To lend, then, or to give, or to do any form of kindness, expecting nothing in return, means that I must settle in my mind that I do not wish to control others with my actions."[3]

I asked God to weed out every last manipulative motive from my heart before Linda's visit, and fill my heart with His unqualified love. It wasn't long before the warm feelings for my friend rekindled and I looked forward enthusiastically to our reunion.

When Linda and her fiancé arrived, the love we all shared was abundant and free. On the final day Linda and I stayed up late into the evening relishing one of our marathon talks. We spoke honestly about our differences (Linda confirmed her decision to leave my church) and then reaffirmed our friendship in the face of the changes that were taking place in her life. Both of us sensed God's Spirit moving on our hearts in a special way, and by the end of the evening it became evident that our friendship had broken through creeds, doctrines, and church affiliations to arrive safely and soundly in the wonderful love of Christ.

For days after our visit I found myself sailing on a spiritual high. Though God had been revealing His unconditional love through experiences with my parents, my husband, my son, and my friend Debra, it was my first experience in expressing that love fully in the face of a serious disagreement with a friend. And by loving Linda without reservation—in spite of our many differences—I sampled a most invigorating draft of God's love.

20

FREE AT LAST

" 'And this is eternal life, that they may know You, the only true God, and Jesus Christ whom You have sent' " (John 17:3, N.K.J.V.).

The differences in Christian beliefs that Linda and I discussed reawakened a raging controversy within my mind that had existed ever since I first caught a glimpse of salvation by faith alone. Apparently, Linda now believed, as many Christians do, that God's law is no longer binding upon our consciences, but I maintained that it is still the Christian's standard for living. My confusion, however, centered upon the relationship between my efforts to obey God's precepts and His free gift of salvation. If, as the Bible clearly teaches, my salvation is wholly dependent upon a faith relationship with Jesus Christ apart from the works or deeds of the law (Romans 3:28), then what role does God's law play in the salvation process? The question had plagued me for years.

My husband tried over and over again to explain the beautiful balance between law and faith, but I could never quite grasp it. I talked with pastors, read books, and prayed, but still came away confused. On the one hand it seemed that the least transgression of God's laws or precepts would cause me to fall from God's grace and erradicate my salvation until I prayed my way back into His graces once again. In other words, one minute salvation was within my grasp and the next minute—after speaking an irritable word—I had lost it. On the other hand, some told me that because obedience to God's law cannot earn my salvation, I should exert no effort in overcoming sin, but simply concentrate on getting to know God through Bible study and prayer. Neither position satisfied my searching soul.

When Linda brought up this controversy once again, I began searching more deeply for the answers. I prayed fervently that I might be able to understand the balance between faith and works once and for all.

One day, after reading several chapters from a tremendous book about man's relationship to Christ entitled *Living: We've Just Begun,* the pieces to my puzzle came hurtling together in one glorious burst of light, freeing me from the last strands of legalism and lifting a tremendous burden of misconceptions from my relationship with God.

In a nutshell I realized that God's law is not an end in itself. God does not ask us to keep it in order to merit salvation (Romans 3:28). Jesus Christ has bought our salvation with His own blood, and as we trust in Him, we are made clean and complete (1 John 1:7; Colossians 2:10). Instead, in His infinite wisdom and love, God has given us His law to reveal those things in our lives that hinder and/or destroy our relationship with Him (Romans 7:7) and that prevent us from revealing His character of love to the world.

Before I discuss the importance of God's law any further, let me stress the vital truth that we cannot even hope to come into harmony with His precepts and principles unless we have His Spirit in our lives. "It is by the Spirit that the heart is made pure. . . . Christ has given His Spirit as a divine power to overcome all hereditary and cultivated tendencies to evil, and to impress His own character upon His church."[1] It is in His Spirit that we must strive to obey, or we will ultimately fail. In practical terms this means spiritually falling at the feet of Jesus every morning, surrendering our own wills, and then inviting His Spirit into our hearts so that we may say along with the apostle Paul, "Not I, but Christ liveth in me" (Galatians 2:20).

But does asking God's Spirit to dwell within us mean that we will have no struggle on our parts? Will Jesus Christ come in and painlessly sweep away all sin from our lives? Will every day be an effortless victory in Christlikeness? Unfortunately, the answer is an emphatic No, for the surrender of our wills to Jesus is the most difficult daily struggle we face, and is crucial to the successful working of His Holy Spirit.

"The battle which we have to fight—the greatest battle that was ever fought by man—is the surrender of self to the will of God, the yielding of the heart to the sovereignty of love. . . . We cannot, of ourselves, conquer the evil desires and habits that strive for the mastery. . . . God alone can give us the victory. . . . But He cannot work in us without our consent and cooperation. The divine Spirit works through the faculties and powers given to man. Our energies are required to cooperate with God."[2]

A surrender means acknowledging our need of God's transforming power in our lives. It involves giving Him all of ourselves, our plans and our desires, and seeking His presence with our whole hearts. A surrender entails cooperating with Him as He seeks to change us into His image of love and allowing Him to remove those things in our lives that keep us from knowing Him more fully. And a full surrender means realizing that everything we do and everything we seek to become as Christians must be accomplished through the agency of His Spirit. (We cannot even surrender without the aid of His Spirit.)

Now, with the understanding that we can come into harmony with God's law only by yielding our wills to Him and allowing His Spirit to live within us, we come back to our original question: What purpose does God's law play in the Christian's life?

Let me emphasize once again that obeying God's law

cannot earn our salvation. Salvation is a free gift from God found only by accepting it and coming into personal relationship with Jesus Christ. " 'And this is eternal life, that they may know You, the only true God, and Jesus Christ whom You have sent' " (John 17:3, N.K.J.V.).

Honoring God's commandments will, however, accomplish two important objectives that I mentioned briefly in the beginning of this chapter—namely, identifying those things that weaken and destroy our relationship with Him, and providing a pattern of God's character to follow as we seek to reveal His love to the world.

Jesus Christ once said, " 'If you keep My commandments, you will abide in My love' " (John 15:10, N.K.J.V.). And one of Christendom's brightest and most prolific writers once penned, "The laws of God are designed to bring His people closer to Himself."[3] In other words, as God enables us to obey His precepts through the agency of His Spirit, we avoid and overcome those attitudes and actions (otherwise known as sins) that interfere with our ability to know Him. Spirit-led obedience roots out attributes contrary to God's nature such as greed, jealousy, and selfishness, and guides us into an ever-deepening relationship with Him.

Let's look at the Ten Commandments in this light. The first commandment asks us not to put any other gods before our Father in heaven. In modern language, it means that we are not to place things like money, sex, or ambition ahead of our relationship with God. For instance, a Christian businessman may be so caught up in making money that he fails to spend any significant time with his Lord. Doing so severs his relationship with God, not because God rejects him, but because he gradually draws away from God. Eventually, if he continues to worship money, he may forget about God entirely—and because salvation centers in knowing God, this would be a fatal step.

The fourth commandment asks us to reserve the seventh day exclusively for God—a day to spend becoming acquainted with Him through nature, worship, Christian service, and family time. Obeying this commandment will greatly enrich our lives through this special association with our God. If we ignore it, however, we may find ourselves lost in the hustle and bustle of life, never fully acknowledging His love or appreciating it for its true worth.

The last commandment asks us not to covet. The word *covet* means to feel an inordinate desire for that which belongs to another. When we covet someone's husband or home or job we do not feel thankful for what God has done in our lives. We do not trust that He knows what is best for us and that His will for our lives will ultimately bring us the greatest happiness. Denying His supreme love for us, we blind ourselves to His true character—again weakening the foundation on which our relationship with Him exists.

Along with the Ten Commandments, God has given us dozens of precepts and principles that also serve to protect us from those things that will hinder us heavenward. Healthful living keeps our minds clear for Bible study and prayer (1 Corinthians 6:19, 20). Patience helps us to wait upon God and listen to His voice (1 Timothy 6:11). Compassion widens our ability to understand His love (1 Peter 3:8). Industry develops our capacity for Christian service (Proverbs 6:6-11). Every principle for living outlined in the Holy Scriptures is designed to open up the way for a more meaningful relationship with God. And, because knowing Him is the key to eternal life, we finally understand why God's precepts and principles are so vital in our Christian experience.

The second objective in allowing God to bring us into harmony with His law concerns our Christian witness. Because God's law is a transcript of His character, it points out those areas in our lives that do not reflect His true personality and reveals those virtues that will make us a shining example of His love.

Just hours ago I witnessed a fascinating solar eclipse. As the moon moved between the sun and the earth, it blocked the sun's powerful rays until, after several minutes, only a small portion of the sun remained visible. I couldn't help thinking of how much sin (transgression of God's law) eclipses our Christian witness to the world. We tell our neighbors of a magnificent Creator, a Saviour able to deliver us from the most captivating sins, and a powerful Lord who changes hearts. But then, instead of backing up our words with a shining example of His love, we allow sin and disobedience to blot out His character in our lives. Backbiting, off-color jokes, covetousness, and jealousy in a Christian's life greatly diminish God's ability to manifest His glorious character to the world, for who's going to believe our story of a magnificent God if we reflect only a mere shadow of His love? On the other hand, the person who allows God's Spirit to bring him into harmony with His law and to transform his character will become a living testimony to the reality of a merciful and all-powerful God.

As we see God's law as a guide to maintaining a healthy relationship with Him and manifesting a true example of His character to the world rather than as a means to earning salvation, we are freed from the law in a legalistic sense but recommitted to it as an essential ingredient in the Christian walk. "Sinlessness [or perfect obedience to God's law] is not an end in itself. It is not, contrary to popular religious opinion, the ultimate spiritual experience. *It is very important because it is the condition needed for intimacy with God.*"[4] Obedience becomes a blessing rather than a burden when we understand that the purpose of our efforts is not to attain heaven, but to enhance and widen our ability to understand and to share God's fathomless love.

This new revelation freed me from the terrible frustration of feeling saved one minute and lost the next. I realized that though I might fail and fumble in my attempts to follow God, it was my growing relationship with Him that secured my salvation. "Mistakes will still be made, behavior may still fall short of perfection, and faults will create waves on the sea of life. But if the set of the will is solidly secured toward seeking daily, intimate oneness with God, the winds of the Spirit will be caught, and the believer will be propelled into the kingdom of God."[5] It also saved me from the temptation to think that the Christian's life requires no kind of effort, for I now saw the vital importance of seeking a daily surrender to Christ and allowing His Spirit to write God's law upon my heart. I understood that everything we do and everything we become as Christians must be accomplished through the agency of His Spirit and motivated by a desire to become intimately acquainted with God.

Not only did my new understanding concerning faith and works free me to pursue a spiritual journey unencumbered by the chains of legalism, but it delivered me from the terrible dilemma of judging others. When we determine our fitness for heaven by our works, we tend to evaluate other people according to their apparent obedience to God's law. But when we realize that salvation is based only on an individual's relationship with Christ—which we cannot fully discern—then we understand that it is impossible to judge fairly and that in fact we are incapable of it at all, for "man looketh on the outward appearance, but the Lord looketh on the heart" (1 Samuel 16:7). Some people who may appear to be missing the mark of righteousness may actually be gaining tremendous victories in areas of their lives that are hidden to our view. And others, whom we define as "hopelessly lost," may actually be responding to God's

Spirit in ways not yet apparent.

To know that it is not our responsibility to judge other human beings leaves us free to love more completely. An unfavorable judgment in the mind leads to a turning away of the heart, but a mind free from criticism and condemnation creates an open channel through which God's love may flow.

My newfound freedom in my relationship with God, His law, and His children unshackled me from fetters of legalism that had bound me for too long. Now, knowing that my great goal is to pursue a growing love relationship with God and my fellowman, I look forward to drinking deeper and deeper drafts of His love.

21

TO DRINK OF HIS LOVE

"If any man thirst, let him come unto me, and drink. He that believeth on me, as the scripture hath said, out of his belly shall flow rivers of living water" (John 7:37, 38).

Ten years have passed since I first dreamed of the golden bottle on the beach containing that one pure golden drop of love. Eight years have gone by since I began my journey to find that love. And now I can honestly say that my dream has come true—or rather, that my dream is just beginning.

I see the pure drop of love as Jesus Christ. And I understand that just to know Him intellectually or to believe simply that He exists can never accomplish my dream's commission to share Him with the world. But, ah, to drink of Him—that is the secret. Then His love will flow forth like streams of living water.

I have only begun to drink of His love. I feel like a child wading at the outskirts of a vast, limitless ocean filled with the water of life. Cupping my hands, I bend down to drink. The water is exhilarating, but I cannot contain much at a time. My capacity is still too limited by scars of yesteryear. But I know Someone who is healing those scars and ever widening my ability to drink and be satisfied.

The more I drink, the more I can share. Unfortunately, I still allow human passions like anger, jealousy, and pride to interrupt the flow from myself to my friends and family. It is a continual struggle against them, but I have a Friend who is fighting the battle with me and winning, slowly but surely.

Ah, to drink of His love. But what does this really mean? How does one actually go about tasting and swallowing the love of God and of His Son, Jesus Christ? What secrets have I learned in the past eight years that I can share with a fellow seeker yet thirsting after life?

First, let me say that to drink of God's love means to experience His love in the depths of our being. It includes experiencing the way He loves both us and our fellowman. Understanding and experiencing God's love is a process of a lifetime, and therefore we cannot expect to receive "instant enlightenment." However, as we apply the following principles to our lives we will develop an ever-increasing capacity to know God.

Before we even begin to know God we must sense our need of Him. Our Father in heaven is working constantly to awaken us to our need, but too often we ignore His wooings. We choose not to consider eternity, but to live for the moment and get the most of this life, whatever the consequences. Sometimes we tell ourselves it is impossible to know God anyway—otherwise, why would there be so many different religions in the world? Other times we fear that if we do seek to know Him, it will lead to all kinds of restrictions on our lives and we will lose all pleasure in living. Day after day we go on ignoring the greatest gift ever bestowed on us—that of communing with and knowing intimately our Maker.

Then one day we sense a stirring within us. Something that we have tried to quiet for five, ten, twenty, or even fifty years cries out once again. It is a need—a need to be connected with a power, perhaps a Being, that is greater than ourselves. A need to rediscover our beginning and to understand our destiny. A need to be loved in a way that we have never been loved before. And on this day, instead of hushing that cry up with pride, pleasure, or new ambitions as we have always done before, we make a decision—a decision to seek God.

Once again we return to our question—How does one actually go about seeking a relationship with God? In my experience I have discovered four main keys to becoming acquainted with Him.

The first involves beholding God in His Holy Scriptures. The Scriptures paint a picture of God that we cannot find anywhere else in this world. The Bible portrays God's love, mercy, care, justice, and magnificence in myriads of ways. By letting our minds dwell upon the wonder of His person, we can be transformed into His image of love—for by beholding, we become changed.

"When the mind of man is brought into communion with the mind of God, the mortal with the immortal, the finite with the infinite, the impact on a person is incredible. In such fellowship is the wellspring of life, the grandest source of inspiration, the highest form of education, the greatest motivation for unselfish love." [1]

The second key involves our private communication with God. Prayer is not just a series of requests that we make to a Sugar Daddy in heaven. We must "desire not merely His blessing, but Himself."[2] It is a deep communing with a loving Being—the Being who created us and knows us more intimately than anyone else in the universe. And prayer is not so much for His benefit as for ours: "Prayer is the opening of the heart to God as to a friend. Not that it is necessary in order to make known to God what we are, but in order to enable us to receive Him."[3]

As we learn to lift our hearts up to God moment by moment, as we learn to thank Him daily for all the wonderful gifts He bestows upon us, and as we learn to place all of our cares before His throne, we will come to sense His presence more vividly each day. And as we continue to invite His Spirit into our hearts, He will speak to us in the most amazing ways, bringing us into deeper and deeper understandings of His love.

Key number three is a vital ingredient in our search to know God, although unfortunately it is an area that many Christians today would rather not emphasize. Our third key entails allowing God to cleanse us of those things that keep us from knowing Him more intimately.

As I've mentioned before, to be filled, we must first be emptied. In order for God to fill us with His love, we must cooperate with Him in removing those actions and attitudes that block Him out. The more we become like Him, the more our capacity will grow for receiving Him into our hearts. "The soul receives and enjoys Him only as it becomes assimilated to Him in character. Only like can appreciate like."[4]

God's Word reveals those things that keep us from knowing Him completely. Of course, we must never think that to seek Him we must first be cleansed, for it is only by coming to God just as we are and receiving His forgiveness that the cleansing process can even begin to take place. After we have surrendered our lives to Him, however, we must allow the purging process to continue.

The fourth key is a dynamic one that never fails to open up floodgates of joy in our lives. It involves asking for God's love so that we may give it to others.

There is nothing more satisfying and nothing more thrilling than to experience the privilege of reaching out to another human being with God's love. When we ask for His love in order to share it, we can be sure that He will answer our prayers, for this is the very heart of Christianity. "It is as we give ourselves to God for the service of humanity that He gives Himself to us."[5]

We need not share His love in dramatic ways like winning dozens of souls to our church or going door-to-door to evangelize, although we can commend those who accomplish such things. Through little things such as home-baked bread, a cheery note card, or a concerned phone call we may find the joy of spreading God's love to the world about us.

The beautiful truth is that when we ask for God's love in order to share it with others, we ourselves will be richly blessed as it flows through our hearts and then outward. Just as a river leaves behind shores laden with budding trees and blossoming flowers, so will God's river of love running through our hearts produce a fertile garden bursting forth with glorious new understandings of Him.

Once again I look back ten years ago to my dream about love, and I want to thank God with all my heart for successfully leading me to His soul-quenching waters of life, despite my stubbornness, pride, and other downfalls. My prayer is for more, Lord, more of Your precious living water. May I continue to kneel at Your feet daily and receive another refreshing draft, for truly I have found that the only way to satisfaction in this life and the only path to eternal salvation in the life to come is to drink ever more deeply of Your wonderful, awe-inspiring love.

References

Chapter 2

*Ellen G. White, *The Desire of Ages* (Mountain View, Calif.: Pacific Press Pub. Assn., 1940), publishers' preface, p. 9.

Chapter 4

*Ellen G. White, *Testimonies for the Church* (Mountain View, Calif.: Pacific Press Pub. Assn., 1948), vol. 5, p. 362.

Chapter 5

*Ellen G. White, *The Ministry of Healing* (Mountain View, Calif.: Pacific Press Pub. Assn., 1942), p. 360.

Chapter 6

[1] *Time*, July 26, 1976, pp. 78, 79.
[2] *Ibid.*, p. 79.
[3] *Ibid.*, p. 78.
[4] *Ibid.*

Chapter 7

[1] White, *The Desire of Ages*, publishers' preface, p. 9.
[2] *Ibid.*, pp. 9, 10.
[3] *Ibid.*, p. 254.

Chapter 8

[1] Ellen G. White, *Thoughts From the Mount of Blessing* (Mountain View, Calif.: Pacific Press Pub. Assn., 1956), p. 123.

[2] The phrase "free gift of salvation" denotes God's promise to pardon, cleanse, and accept fully the sinner through the merits of Jesus Christ alone, and not by any works or efforts on the sinner's part.

[3] "Saved" is a common expression in Christianity used to describe a believer's acceptance with God and assurance of eternal life.

[4] To "lose my salvation" would be to forfeit my right standing before God and thus my eternal life.

[5] An erroneous belief exists in some Christian circles that our salvation depends upon our perfect obedience, and that each time we err we fall away from God's grace. The Bible clearly teaches, however, that although we are to strive for perfection, the perfection that qualifies us for heaven we find in Christ alone and not in ourselves.

Chapter 9

*White, *The Ministry of Healing*, p. 469.

Chapter 10

* White, *The Desire of Ages*, p. 22.

Chapter 11

*Ellen G. White, *Steps to Christ* (Mountain View, Calif.: Pacific Press Pub. Assn., 1956), p. 68.

Chapter 12

[1] Ellen G. White, *The Adventist Home* (Nashville, Tenn.: Southern Pub. Assn., 1952), p. 51.

[2] *Ibid.*, p. 71.

[3] *Ibid.*, pp. 44, 45.

Chapter 13

[1] White, *Steps to Christ*, p. 52.

[2] *Ibid.*, p. 47.

[3] ———, *Christ's Object Lessons* (Washington, D.C.: Review and Herald Pub. Assn., 1941), p. 65.

Chapter 14

*White, *The Ministry of Healing*, pp. 480, 481.

Chapter 16

[1] White, *Thoughts From the Mount of Blessing*, p. 128.

[2] After this change we no longer had any direct connection with the self-supporting community in which we originally met, but were now employed by the local conference of our denomination.

[3] ———, *The Desire of Ages*, p. 357.

[4] ———, *Patriarchs and Prophets* (Mountain View, Calif.: Pacific Press Pub. Assn., 1958), pp. 247-252.

Chapter 17

[1] White, *The Adventist Home*, p. 160.

[2] *Ibid.*

Chapter 18

*White, *Thoughts From the Mount of Blessing*, p. 137.

Chapter 19

[1] Dick Winn, "Is God Disappointed With Us?" *Weimar News*, January, 1984, p. 8.

[2] Ellen G. White, *The Acts of the Apostles* (Mountain View, Calif.: Pacific Press Pub. Assn., 1911), p. 541.

[3] Winn, *op. cit.*, p. 8.

Chapter 20

[1] White, *The Desire of Ages*, p. 671.

[2] ———, *Thoughts From the Mount of Blessing*, pp. 141, 142.

[3] ———, *Testimonies for the Church*, vol. 5, p. 45.

[4] Douglas Cooper, *Living: We've Just Begun* (Mountain View, Calif.:

Pacific Press Pub. Assn., 1983), p. 80.
[5] *Ibid.*, p. 46.

Chapter 21
[1] Cooper, *Living: We've Just Begun,* p. 84.
[2] White, *Thoughts From the Mount of Blessing,* p. 131.
[3] ———, *Steps to Christ,* p. 93.
[4] ———, *Thoughts From the Mount of Blessing,* p. 81.
[5] *Ibid.*